The Real Sherlock Holmes

The Real Sherlock Holmes

The Hidden Story of Jerome Caminada

Angela Buckley

PEN & SWORD HISTORY

First published in Great Britain in 2014 by
Pen & Sword History
an imprint of
Pen & Sword Books Ltd
47 Church Street
Barnsley
South Yorkshire
S70 2AS

ISBN 978 1 78159 269 4

A CIP catalogue record for this book is available from the British
Library

Typeset in Ehrhardt by
Mac Style, Bridlington, East Yorkshire
Printed and bound in the UK by CPI Group (UK) Ltd, Croydon,
CRO 4YY

Pen & Sword Books Ltd incorporates the imprints of Pen & Sword
Archaeology, Atlas, Aviation, Battleground, Discovery, Family History,
History, Maritime, Military, Naval, Politics, Railways, Select,
Transport, True Crime, and Fiction, Frontline Books, Leo Cooper,
Praetorian Press, Seaforth Publishing and Wharncliffe.

For a complete list of Pen & Sword titles please contact
PEN & SWORD BOOKS LIMITED
47 Church Street, Barnsley, South Yorkshire, S70 2AS, England
E-mail: enquiries@pen-and-sword.co.uk
Website: www.pen-and-sword.co.uk

For Warren

'Cant as we may,' said the immortal Dickens, 'we shall to the end of all things find it very much harder for the poor to be virtuous than it is for the rich, and the good that is in them shines the brighter for it.'

(Jerome Caminada, *Twenty-Five Years of Detective Life*, 1895)

Contents

Preface

My journey into Victorian Manchester's criminal underworld began with my own family. During a break from my full-time teaching career, I needed a project to keep my brain active, so I began researching my family history. All families have skeletons in their genealogical cupboard and it wasn't long before mine started rattling loudly. Even though they committed mostly petty crimes – theft, drunkenness and criminal damage – I was fascinated by my dubious ancestors and soon the wider nineteenth century tempted me in.

After considerable research into Victorian crime and several published articles on the subject, I never expected to find myself writing my first book from the perspective of a law enforcer, but Caminada came also from the pages of my family's history. In the mid-1880s, my great-great-grandparents, Michele and Maria Coppola, made the long and arduous journey from the sun-drenched fields of Italy to the grey, sodden slums of Ancoats, Manchester. One of the most prominent members of the city's lively expatriate Italian community was Detective Inspector Jerome Caminada.

My curiosity aroused, I undertook my own investigation into Detective Caminada's career. Following him into the dark streets of Manchester during the 1870s and 1880s, I encountered nefarious criminals of all kinds – desperate thieves, convincing charlatans and clever con artists. I learned about forgery, street fighting, poisoning and the heinous crime of infanticide. Furthermore, I joined social commentators such as Friedrich Engels, in gambling dens, gin palaces and brothels in the dingy alleyways of my home city's past.

My research into the nineteenth century reached full circle with a remarkable discovery in my own family's past. I was tracing my three times great-grandfather, John Dawson, and when I located him in Manchester on the 1861 census I couldn't believe my eyes. In tiny spidery handwriting over John's entry, the enumerator had added, 'Keeps a house of infamous notoriety'. Further study revealed that my ancestor had been convicted several times for 'keeping a disorderly house' and even spent time in

Strangeways Prison. In a startling coincidence, John Dawson's house of ill repute was on the beat of young Police Constable Jerome Caminada, when he joined the force in 1868. I have yet to find evidence of them meeting, but they must have known each other, and I like to think they did.

When Jerome Caminada died in 1914, his colleague and friend Judge Parry said, during his eulogy, that 'someone will no doubt, in due course edit some proper record' of the detective's adventures. A century later, using Caminada's own memoirs, supplemented by contemporary records and newspaper accounts, I have attempted to reconstruct his unique story. He was a man of strong opinions and resolute intentions and I hope that, after decades of silence, the voice of this extraordinary Victorian super-sleuth will be heard once again.

Angela Buckley, 2013

Prologue

Monday 6 December 1886

At 11pm on a cold winter's evening, the doors of the Queen's Theatre on Bridge Street, Manchester, swung open and the buzzing throng spilled out into the dank, smoky streets. Well-heeled gentlemen jostled through the crowds, holding on to their hats as the wind blew in icy squalls. Women muffled in coats and scarves clutched the arms of their companions, their heady perfume masking the tang of detritus and human waste flowing in the gutters of the filthy streets nearby.

Amongst this teeming mass was 33-year-old Arthur Foster, a smartly dressed and clean-shaven man with the air of an actor. Some said that he resembled the celebrated star of the stage, Henry Irving. Standing proud, this attractive man had a beautiful woman on his arm. She was bedecked in jewels, with a magnificent cat's diamond bracelet adorning her wrist. Foster breathed in the freezing air and with a satisfied sigh, cast a glance over the road at the private brougham waiting for them as planned. Leaving the shelter of the theatre's stone canopy, the handsome couple pushed their way through the crowd. All around them theatre-goers with red cheeks scanned the street for a vacant cab to take them safely back to their elegant townhouses and suburban villas.

The shops were closed, but hawkers and street-sellers hung around in the shadows, offering passersby a last chance to buy cheap household wares; matches, twine and corset laces. Food stalls were being packed away, leaving a few shrivelled hot potatoes and penny pies for those who had not been tempted by the ham sandwiches sold at the theatre door. At the end of the street coffee sellers were setting up their stalls for the midnight trade, accompanied by the lugubrious tune of a lone organ grinder. The seedy public houses and gin palaces tucked away in the nearby labyrinth of alleys and dirty streets had yet to relinquish their customers, but the shouts of tipsy men spoiling for a fight rumbled beneath the chatter of the crowds.

Like everyone around them, Foster and his lady friend ignored the pinched, pale faces of the shabby women hanging about on the grubby kerb stones, hoping to earn a few pence by entertaining a gentleman before he went home. The couple had enjoyed a pleasant evening at a performance of *The World*, a Drury Lane drama in which the police hunt a jewellery thief after he steals some valuable diamonds. The woman was no stranger to the theatre. Known as the 'Vanishing Lady', she was currently appearing at the Free Trade Hall, but this evening a disappointed audience had been informed that she was 'indisposed'.

Now their hired brougham pulled up alongside the pavement, the horses flicking their tails and snorting warm steam into the frosty night. Foster stepped back to guide his companion into the cab, before climbing in beside her. As they settled down on the upholstered bench, the coachman gently cracked his whip. The carriage lurched forward and then stopped abruptly, jolting the passengers on their seat. Before Foster could call out, the door opened and a shadowy figure slipped inside. The yellow light of a gas lamp revealed him as an older man, dark-haired, with a full beard and moustache. Removing his hat, he apologised for the intrusion and asked politely if he could join them. At first bewildered and then indignant, Foster opened his mouth to protest, but fell silent as he recognised the stranger. Catching his breath, he made a dash for one door whilst his companion dived towards the other. The intruder blocked his exit and another man was waiting outside, ready to prevent their escape. Foster was trapped; there was no way out. He sank back into the bench as the Vanishing Lady sobbed hysterically beside him.

Arthur Foster, also known as the Birmingham Forger, was wanted by the police for theft and a serious fraud amounting to £5,200. The intruder sitting in his cab was Detective Chief Inspector Jerome Caminada, who had once again caught his man.

Unbeknown to Foster, Detective Chief Inspector Caminada had been shadowing him since noon. The thief had led the detective a merry dance through the streets and main squares of the bustling city, without Foster once realising that he was being tracked. The chase had begun at the Bank of England on the fashionable boulevard of King Street, right in the centre of Manchester. Surrounded by glittering shop windows and exclusive boutiques, the police officer had been standing near the bank when he spotted a suspicious-looking man loitering by the imposing red brick building. Recognising him from a picture circulated by the Birmingham force, Caminada knew instantly that he was looking at the wanted forger, Arthur Foster.

Foster, who used a number of aliases, had already served 10 years in prison for a similar theft. Now he was back in circulation and doing rather well. The detective slipped into the bank behind his quarry and followed him to the bullion office, where Foster changed a large amount of gold into notes. After leaving the bank, he trailed the suspect into another bank further along the street, where he repeated the transaction.

Together they criss-crossed the commercial centre, with Foster visiting a number of money-changers and Caminada following carefully in his wake. After passing through several streets, they reached St Ann's Square, where Foster hailed a cab from the rank and took off again in the direction of Deansgate, the main thoroughfare behind the square. Jumping into the next cab behind Foster, the chief inspector tailed him to Bridge Street and watched while the suspect entered the Queen's Theatre, where he reserved a private box for that evening. On the road again and his errands completed, Foster drove out to Greenheys, a less salubrious suburb just two miles from the city centre, where gloomy textile mills overshadowed grimy, smoke-blackened terrace houses. The hansom dropped him off at his lodgings, at 53 Carter Street, while Caminada watched him in the dark.

At 6pm that evening Foster was on the move again, travelling by cab back towards the city with Caminada in pursuit at a discreet distance. Stopping briefly en route at a lodging house for theatrical ladies, he collected his female companion for the evening performance at the Queen's Theatre, blissfully unaware that the detective was lying in wait.

Arthur Foster had become over-confident after recently evading capture in London and Birmingham, but he could not defy the determination of Chief Inspector Caminada. The arrest would result in a heist of gold and jewellery worth almost three quarters of a million pounds today, being recovered single-handedly by the indefatigable investigator.

When he arrested the Birmingham Forger, Jerome Caminada had been policing the crime-ridden rookeries of inner city Manchester for almost two decades and he knew all about criminals and their nefarious ways. Dubbed by the *Evening Telegraph* a 'terror to evil doers', he was reputed to be able to spot a thief by the way he walked and sniff out a swindle from a considerable distance. An expert at deduction, he was a force to be reckoned with. In 1886, a year before his fictional counterpart, Sherlock Holmes, made his debut in *A Study in Scarlet*, 42-year-old Caminada was at the top of his game. In the months leading up to Foster's arrest, he had exposed a number of major frauds, including bogus heir hunters, quack doctors and a sophisticated emigration scam.

During the next few years, Caminada would become renowned throughout the country, as he captured an escaped political prisoner, confronted a deadly career criminal and played a pivotal role in the nationwide hunt for the Fenian dynamite conspirators. Using methods worthy of the iconic consulting detective himself, Caminada would tackle his most baffling case yet: 'The Manchester Cab Mystery'.

Despite a personal life beset with tragedy, this legendary detective would remain resolute in his fight against crime and earn his place in the city's history as one of its finest detectives. Jerome Caminada was a true Victorian super-sleuth and a real-life Sherlock Holmes.

Chapter One

'A very hot-bed of social iniquity and vice'
(1844–1868)

One Sunday the Bishop of Salford, Herbert Vaughan, was leaving St Augustine's Church in Manchester after Mass, when a swell mobsman (a well-dressed, highly skilled pickpocket) made a daring attempt to snatch his magnificent pectoral cross, while his hands were raised in the act of blessing his flock. The thief would have succeeded – had Jerome Caminada not been in the congregation. In an instant, before the bishop had realised what was happening, the detective had retrieved the cross. Despite having chosen the police force over the priesthood, Caminada's religious faith and childhood experiences had a significant impact on his future and would influence his remarkable crime-fighting career for more than three decades.

Caminada's early life could not have been more different to the history of his literary peer, Sherlock Holmes. When Dr Watson questioned the provenance of the consulting detective's faculties of observation and deduction in 'The Adventure of the Greek Interpreter', Holmes admitted that some of his skills may have come from his family history:

My ancestors were country squires, who appear to have led much the same life as is natural to their class. But, none the less, my turn that way is in my veins, and may have come with my grandmother, who was the sister of Vernet, the French artist. Art in the blood is liable to take the strangest forms.

By comparison, Jerome Caminada did not come from the landed gentry or have a university education, but his ability to solve complicated cases bore an uncanny similarity to the exceptional skills of the famous 'sleuth-hound', and was also rooted in his past.

Jerome Caminada was born to immigrant parents on 15 March 1844 in Deansgate, opposite the site of the infamous Peterloo Massacre. In the 1840s, Manchester was one of the poorest and most dangerous places in Britain. With some of the nation's worst living conditions and staggering crime rates, life for manual workers was an uphill struggle. Since the opening of the first mill by Richard Arkwright in 1780, the city had seen unprecedented change. The cotton industry had burgeoned beyond expectation, accelerated by the development of an effective transport system – first the canals and later the railways – and, by the early nineteenth century, 'Cottonopolis' was established as the world's first industrial city. But whilst industrialisation brought tremendous wealth to Manchester's factory owners and businessmen, for thousands of others penned into the notorious slums of the city, life was tougher than ever.

During the first half of the nineteenth century, the number of inhabitants of Manchester had tripled, reaching 242,000 in 1841, as migrant workers poured into the city to try their luck in the factories and mills. Inadequate housing stock forced them to live in cramped accommodation, without clean water and basic amenities. It was in these filthy streets, and with the odds stacked against him, that Caminada fought to survive a precarious childhood. In his memoirs he described the contrast that characterised Victorian Manchester: 'In this great city, we have, side by side with enormous wealth and luxury, an inconceivable amount of squalor, misery, degradation, and filthiness of life'.

The families of both Jerome's parents were among the mass of immigrants who flocked to Manchester for work at the turn of the nineteenth century. In the early 1800s, skilled craftsmen migrated to England from northern Italy, settling in towns and cities throughout the country. Manchester was now home to a number of Italian businesses, which made precision instruments such as thermometers, telescopes and magnifying glasses. Jerome's paternal grandfather, Lewis Caminada, was a barometer-maker. Originally from Lombardy in northern Italy, he arrived in Manchester in the late 1700s. His son, Francis, (Jerome's father) was born in the city around 1811. Francis followed his father into a skilled trade and became a cabinetmaker.

Detective Caminada retained his mixed cultural heritage throughout his life: 'He was in appearance a typical Italian with very strongly marked features, but he never lost his native Lancashire speech, and was in many ways very much a Lancashire man until the end of his days' (*Daily Mail*). Caminada's mother, Mary Boyle, although born in Glasgow, had Irish roots and her father, Cornelius Boyle, was a mechanic. Mary was also from an impoverished background and, like many others before the Education Act of 1870 introduced compulsory schooling, she had never learned to read or write.

Francis and Mary Caminada's first child was born in 1837. By the early 1840s, the couple had settled in Deansgate, central Manchester. Luxurious shops, magnificent hotels and bustling streets dominated the city's commercial district, but close by the grand façades were smoking factories, grimy warehouses and tenements. The journalist Angus Bethune Reach gave a description of the area in the *Morning Chronicle*: 'between the dull stacks of warehouses and the snug and airy dwellings of the suburbs – lies the great mass of smoky, dingy, sweltering and toiling Manchester'.

The major thoroughfare of Deansgate, which ran through the heart of the city, was lined with mills and warehouses, but as the road left the business district, second-rate shops, alehouses and gin palaces soon replaced them. On both sides of Deansgate were the inner-city slums, where poverty was endemic and crime rife. Caminada later recalled the streets of his childhood: 'The neighbourhood of Deansgate also was the rendezvous of thieves and was a very hot-bed of social iniquity and vice'.

The 1841 census records Francis and Mary Caminada, aged 30 and 25 respectively, living with their three young children: Francis, aged three; John Baptiste, two; and Hannah, one, in a house shared with four other families. There would have been no running water and the 13 inhabitants of the house shared an outside privy with the other residents of the street. The couple were unmarried, but later that year, they finally tied the knot at St Augustine's Roman Catholic Church, in nearby Granby Row. By this time they had moved around the corner to 33 Peter Street, opposite the Free Trade Hall, which commemorates the 1819 Peterloo Massacre, when the Manchester Yeomanry fired on innocent protestors, killing at least 11 and injuring more than 600.

Peter Street was a mixed area, with two-storey terrace houses sitting shoulder to shoulder with public buildings. There were warehouses, timber yards and smaller dwellings, as well as theatres, concert halls and the original Manchester Museum. It was also well known for brothels and illegal drinking dens. The *Manchester Evening News* stated that, 'The Peter-street side of Deansgate once shared with the Wood-street neighbourhood the questionable notoriety of being the most dangerous district in the city', with 'beerhouses in which nightly assembled lawless characters of the worst type'. Despite this reputation, Francis and Mary stayed there for the births of their three younger children, Louis in 1842, followed by Jerome in 1844 and Teresa in 1846.

In the first of a series of tragic events for the Caminada family, baby Louis died aged nine months, of 'hydrocephalus acutus', a disease of the brain. Then four years later, three-year-old Jerome's eldest brother, Francis, aged nine, died of enteritis. The health of children growing up in industrial Manchester at that time was notoriously poor. Overcrowding, inadequate sanitation and contaminated water contributed to the shockingly high infant mortality rate: in the 1840s, 48 per cent of all recorded deaths in Manchester were of children under five years old, with the majority dying before their first birthday. Many of these untimely deaths were attributed to childhood diseases like small pox and scarlet fever, as well as diarrhoea from infected water supplies.

Adults too were at risk of disease due to the appalling conditions and a lack of basic medical care. Just two months after the death of his eldest brother, Jerome Caminada's fragile childhood was completely shattered when his father, Francis, died of heart disease at the age of 37. Some time after Francis's death, the remaining members of the Caminada family moved to Quay Street, on the other side of Deansgate. Tucked away behind the main road, this area of atrocious slums was a warren of dirty tenements and disreputable lodging-houses. Friedrich Engels depicted the streets around Quay Street in *The Condition of the Working Class in England in 1844*:

> *Here are long, narrow lanes between which run contracted, crooked courts and passages, the entrances to which are so irregular that the explorer is caught in a blind alley at every few steps...the most demoralised class in all Manchester lived in these ruinous and filthy districts, people whose occupations are thieving and prostitution.*

Although once a fashionable quarter, the area had deteriorated and the two-storey houses, now sheltering the city's poorest residents, were dilapidated and shabby. Behind Quay Street were rows of poorly ventilated and tightly packed back-to-back houses, which shared water pumps and privies between at least 20 households. The dense black smoke of the factory chimneys and the stench of rotting refuse permeated the unpaved streets, full of stagnant cesspools and open pigsties.

The soot-blackened terrace houses were made of crumbling brick, their broken windows stuffed with rags and paper in a vain attempt to keep out the driving rain and cold wind. The worst type of housing was the 'one-up-one-down'. Each room housed at least one family but, more often than not, several families were living cramped together in the confined space. The most unfortunate were forced to live underground in the cellars.

Inside these ramshackle dwellings were minimal amenities: a fireplace for cooking and maybe a few sticks of cheap furniture. Some slept on thin mattresses, but others had to make do with rags or straw. The walls were damp and often bare. No stranger to these surroundings, Caminada gave a detailed description of the conditions in his memoirs: 'the atmosphere being nothing but a fetid composition of pestilential vapour emitted from filthy beds, dirty clothing, foul breath, and, worse than all, the presence of offensive matter in the room'.

Many workers in Manchester's mills and factories lived a hand-to-mouth existence. Average weekly wages in the early 1840s were around 10 shillings, half of which would be needed for the rent. Some operatives, such as spinners, earned higher wages and enjoyed better living conditions, but most families relied on the income of several members. The situation was particularly precarious for those affected by illness or the loss of the male provider and the poorest workers wore threadbare clothing and rarely had enough food to eat. Engels recounted how those who did not even possess a hat, would fold a piece of paper into a makeshift cap. Starvation and cold were constant threats to survival.

Despite such gruelling circumstances, the Caminadas fared relatively well, at first. In 1851, just four years after the death of her husband, Mary was letting out rooms in the lodging-house where she also lived with her four surviving children. The going rate for a bed for the night in 1849 was four pence and she had three lodgers. The young family was quite settled, with Jerome, aged six, and his siblings all attending St Mary's Roman Catholic School, just a few streets away from their home. It was a small school run by nuns and most of the children were of Irish descent. In a rare reference to his childhood, Caminada later reminisced: 'I remember, when a youth, writing in my copy book "Evil companions corrupt morals," and there is no doubt about the truth of it'.

The family worshipped at St Mary's Roman Catholic Church, Mulberry Street, where Jerome had been baptised. Still known today as the Hidden Gem, the city centre church, with its beautiful white marble altar, is concealed by office blocks and commercial buildings. As a police detective, Caminada allegedly used to meet his informers on the back pew, giving the impression that he was praying, whilst discussing his business quietly in the silence of the church.

However, by 1853 the family had lost their battle to escape the worst of the slums and were living in Little Quay Street. A reporter for the *Manchester Evening News* described the quarter some 20 years later:

*In Little Quay-street the class of persons also appeared to be of the lowest of
the hard-working population, and in some of the courts the scanty furniture
and the squalid appearance of the kitchens showed how hard was the struggle
for existence. Being Saturday night many of the women were washing linen
for the Sabbath, and across the rooms were stretched clothes-lines, on which
ragged shirts and well-worn underclothing were slowly drying.*

That winter Mary gave birth to a boy named Lewis and this event may have
accounted for the family's move. His father's name was not recorded. On
Christmas Day the infant died of unknown causes, aged just five weeks.

Five years on the family had fallen even further into chaos. In 1858 Mary
had another son, also called Lewis. This time the father was registered as
John Boyd, a stonemason. When the baby died three months later, his death
certificate revealed a shocking truth: the cause of death was 'congenital
syphilis'. Syphilis was rife in Victorian England and, as it was difficult to
diagnose, it is not known how many victims this devastating disease claimed.
Entering into the bloodstream through sexual contact, the infection was
also passed from a mother to her unborn child, resulting in stillbirth, birth
defects and early death. Infants with congenital syphilis suffered damage
to their bones, teeth, ears, eyes and worst of all, to the developing brain.
Even if syphilitic children survived early infancy, symptoms could appear
at any time, affecting their neurological and cardiovascular systems and
often resulting in blindness, deafness or mental illness. Before the advent of
antibiotics, the situation was hopeless.

In the Caminada family, it is impossible to say conclusively how many of
Jerome's siblings may have contracted syphilis through their mother. Eight
months after the death of baby Lewis, and once again on Christmas Day,
15-year-old Hannah Caminada died in Crumpsall Workhouse. The recorded
causes of death were 'idiocy', tuberculosis and diarrhoea. The reference to
her mental deterioration makes it likely that the disease had affected her
too. The informant on Hannah's death certificate was her younger brother,
Jerome, aged just 14.

By his early teens Jerome Caminada had witnessed the deaths of five close
relatives. Although unimaginable today, such a high death rate in one family
was almost to be expected in the Victorian era, especially with the recurrent
epidemics of contagious diseases, such as cholera and typhoid, which swept
through communities. Nevertheless, the strain on Mary Caminada and
her three surviving children must have been considerable. Despite these
tragic setbacks, they managed to salvage what they could from their meagre

existence and in 1861 they were still living in a shared household, but now with only one other family. Their circumstances had improved because the children were all working. Mary was now 48 and Jerome 17. Teresa, aged 14, was employed as a silk weaver, probably in a local factory and Mary's eldest living son, John Baptiste, 20, was lodging in Newcastle upon Lyme, where he was working as a letter carrier.

After leaving school, Jerome spent six years in the Royal Lancashire Militia, before finding work as a brass-fitter. In the 1860s he was employed by two manufacturing companies. The first was Messrs Sharp and Stewart, a steam locomotive manufacturer responsible for building one of the first locomotives to travel on the Liverpool and Manchester Railway. He then worked for Messrs Mather and Platt, a large engineering firm which owned the Salford Ironworks. Work in a foundry was dirty, hot and noisy. Beating hammers, roaring furnaces and dense smoke would have made the conditions almost unbearable for the workers, who were engaged in backbreaking physical labour. Endless days of toiling in the sweltering heat of the ironworks may have been one of the factors that influenced Caminada in his momentous decision to become a police officer. On 20 February 1868, at the age of 23, Jerome Caminada joined the Manchester City Police Force as a police constable.

Detective Caminada's first-hand knowledge of the city's back streets and the people who lived there, would be an effective weapon in his daily battle against crime. 'The rookeries of the city had no terrors for him', declared the *Manchester Courier* years later, 'although, on many occasions, he deliberately ran grave risks in order to accomplish his object – the arrest of criminals'. His training in the militia and the physical nature of his work in the foundry had given him stamina, strength and a sense of discipline. Furthermore, his early experiences of poverty and hardship had instilled in him a deep sense of justice and a heartfelt compassion for others.

Jerome Caminada had served his 'apprenticeship' in the seedy and violent slums of his childhood. In 1868, as his life of fighting crime began, young PC Caminada would need all his faith, courage and determination to face the challenges that awaited him on the streets of Manchester's dark underworld.

Chapter Two

'A "Lively" Beat'
(1868–1871)

A policeman seldom forgets his first nights on duty. If he be an intelligent officer he feels that he is a person of some importance, that a large responsibility is placed upon his shoulders in looking after the safety of the lives and property of the Queen's subjects on his beat, and in vindicating the laws of his country. He has visions of future promotion, and being anxious to distinguish himself, his eyes and ears are on the alert to everything that passes around, for he is in search of his first case. Thus his novitiate is full of excitement, especially if he be on a "lively" beat.

(Jerome Caminada, *Twenty-Five Years of Detective Life*, 1901)

These were Police Constable Caminada's noble sentiments as he prepared to patrol the streets of his neighbourhood for the very first time. By the end of the week, he had been ridiculed, insulted and assaulted. With dented pride, but unabated enthusiasm, he later conceded that 'a policeman's life is not altogether a bed of roses'.

Prior to the formation of the Manchester Borough Watch Committee in 1839, each township was responsible for its own policing, which was mostly carried out by day and night watchmen and relied on military intervention when necessary. The new police force was established in Manchester in 1842, following the appointment of the city's first chief commissioner three years earlier. Initially the force comprised 398 police officers, who served a population of 242,000. Most of the recruits were young and inexperienced like Caminada, and they received a salary of 17 shillings a week, which, although a regular wage at the time, was barely adequate to support a family. By the time Caminada joined the Manchester City Police Force in 1868, the salary of a police constable had increased to £1 1s 6d. The number of officers had also doubled and they were now separated into five divisions.

Caminada was attached to A Division under Chief Superintendent John Gee, known as the 'Gentle Shepherd' because of his 'loud voice and boisterous manner'. A Division's headquarters was at Knott Mill Police Station in Deansgate. PC Caminada was 5 feet 8 inches tall, just meeting the height entry requirements. He had a fresh complexion, grey eyes and brown hair and when he set out on his beat for the first time, he would have been wearing the official dark blue tunic with his service number A21 marked on his collar. The uniform was neither waterproof nor warm, and inadequate for the damp, freezing conditions in the northwest of England. He wore a helmet, which had replaced the distinctive 'stovepipe' top hat in 1865 and on his thick leather belt hung a pair of handcuffs, a wooden truncheon and rattle.

Caminada's main duty was to 'walk the beat', patrolling a small area of the city for 14 hours a day, at the regulation pace of two-and-a-half miles an hour. He had to meet his sergeant at fixed points along the route to pass on information about incidents and public disturbances. He was also required to watch out for fires, check all doors and windows, and to help the general public when necessary. Caminada was allocated to No 7 Beat, covering the slums of Quay Street, Byrom Street, Cupid's Alley and Hardman Street. This rookery had hardly changed since he had lived there as a child and, despite the best efforts of the local police force, violence and lawlessness reigned in the dingy labyrinthine streets.

In March 1869, the Reverend Alfred Alsop, founder of the Wood Street Mission in Deansgate, undertook a study of the locality and published a graphic description of the inhabitants in his book, *Ten Years in the Slums* (1876):

> *The stamp of iniquity is impressed upon all, both young and old. It is all filth, dirt, rags, poverty, squalor, swearing, drunkenness, theft, broken windows, smashed doors, creaking stairs, bad smells, bare rooms, shattered furniture, black eyes, broken heads, bleeding faces, brutal fights, heathenish cruelty, unwashed children, wretched babies, besotted mothers, sluggish fathers, shameless sisters, and pocket-picking, shop-lifting brothers.*

Even during the daytime the main thoroughfares of the city were populated by all manner of criminals – from gangs of thieves and professional beggars to ruthless con artists and nimble pickpockets. On street corners and in the doorways of public houses, were 'sharps' (swindlers) and 'magsmen' (cheats) waiting to accost innocent passersby and encourage them to part with their hard earned cash. Fake sailors, out-of-work colliers and crippled ex-soldiers, returning from foreign climes, reached out their arms to passing 'swells' (gentlemen), their pinched faces lined with pain and hardship, as they recounted their sorrowful tales. Few of them had ever seen the sea, fought on a battlefield or toiled down a mine, but all were adept at spinning a convincing story. Nearby, ragged women sat in huddles with 'hired' children wrapped in their threadbare skirts, as they implored shoppers to spare them a penny.

Skilled con artists operated all kinds of tricks and scams on the streets of the city. 'Dry land' sailors even sold 'smuggled' treasure from shipwrecks. In one popular con a man would fall to the ground in an epileptic fit, frothing at the mouth (a simple effect created by soap), until a sympathetic bystander handed him a coin for a drink to calm his twitching limbs. Well-dressed 'mobsmen' mingled with the unsuspecting crowd to relieve the wealthy of their wallets and watches. Amongst the thieves and cadgers, were multitudes of street tradespeople or 'land-sharks', plying their shoddy goods from the pavement – stolen clothing, fake jewellery and cheap merchandise – the smoky air ringing with their plaintive shouts for business.

More dangerous still were women with tears in their eyes and torn skirts, who would cry for help and beckon a gentleman away from the throng to assist them, or prostitutes tempting them into the shadows. Before he knew it, the unwary gentleman would be attacked and robbed by the 'coshers' (thugs) waiting in the dark.

Official police returns confirmed the high levels of crime on the streets of Victorian Manchester. In 1866, there were some 13,000 arrests, with robbery and pickpocketing being the most common crimes. By 1870, the number of arrests had doubled. Indictable offences (i.e. those brought to trial) included assault, breach of the peace, drunkenness, stealing and prostitution. The crime rate in Manchester was almost two crimes per person – four times higher than in London during the same period. Only five per cent of these arrests resulted in conviction. PC Caminada had his work cut out.

Late one evening in March 1868, Caminada stepped out with pride in his new uniform ready to tackle the crime-infested streets of his neighbourhood. It was a freezing cold night with snow on the ground and, as he picked his way along the slippery pavements of John Dalton Street in the pale, yellow light of the gas lamps, a man called out to him. When Caminada turned to face him, he was assailed by a tirade of insults: 'Have I to pay rates and taxes to keep such lazy fellows as you walking about the streets?' Before the young policeman had a chance to respond to this unprovoked attack the man, a beerhouse-keeper named Quinn, punched him in the face, and fled the scene.

'I was certainly a little non-plussed', Caminada recollected, 'To get a violent blow on the nose… was not a very pleasant experience for a beginner'. Undeterred, he returned to his business of pacing the beat, but as he reached the corner of the street he suddenly received another thump from Quinn, this time to his ear, accompanied by the words, 'Take that! How do you like it?'

Still smarting from the blow, Caminada pursued the beerhouse-keeper as he took off into the night. Quinn flew up a flight of stairs leading into a nearby tavern, but Caminada grabbed his legs and dragged him back down to the pavement. A scuffle ensued, which resulted in Quinn biting the policeman's hand 'in right good fashion'. Luckily the injury was not as serious as it might have been: 'Fortunately, he had no teeth, but he worked away so vigorously with his gums that I could feel the pain for weeks after'. Quinn was convicted of assault and Caminada never forgot his first incidence of violence as an officer: 'Though the matter was no joke at the time, I often smile when I come across my friend, the beerhouse-keeper, Quinn'.

After a challenging week, Caminada's first Saturday night on duty was no better. Snow was ankle-deep on the pavements as PC Caminada prepared to face another freezing night on duty:

as I stood in the steady downfall, with the cold about zero, eating my supper, the outlook on that bitter Saturday night was not particularly cheering. Anxious, however, to distinguish myself, I had no time to moralise, so "bolting" my supper in the best way possible under such circumstances, I again commenced to patrol my beat with all the importance of a newly-made policeman.

Passing the 'dirty narrow gullet' of Thompson Street he heard a 'row' coming from a common lodging-house, the home of James Woodcock, alias Jimmy Good-lodgings, his wife and their three sons. The family had been 'holding high carnival' and as Caminada lifted the latch the noise grew louder. Jimmy and his wife were sitting by the fire singing, dancing and cursing, while the youngest son was drunkenly muttering to himself on a chair. The room was full of old-fashioned country furniture, including a large sofa draped in check calico, with a valance hanging down at the front to obscure the sight of the family's shoes stored underneath. A scuffling noise 'resembling that of a dog fight' was coming from underneath the sofa drapes and on closer inspection, Caminada found the two older sons fighting underneath it, both drunk and 'worrying each other like a pair of bulldogs'.

Caminada dragged them out: 'I shall never forget the appearance they presented. Their hands and feet were so bruised and bitten, that there was scarcely a spot as large as a sixpence which did not bear marks of savage brutality'. He threatened the whole family with arrest if they didn't stop their violent behaviour, but he did not quite get the reaction he had hoped for: 'I very soon found that whatever opinion I had of my own importance, neither the uniform nor the "little brief authority" of the newly-made policeman had any terror for these fiends'. The two brothers quickly settled their differences and then joined forces to defy their 'common enemy', setting on the policeman and demanding to know who had sent for him and what he was doing there. Worried about ending up under the sofa himself, Caminada decided that 'discretion was the better part of valour' and backed into the street as the door was slammed firmly behind him. But the evening was not over yet.

He had just resumed his beat in the falling snow, when he heard cries of 'Murder!' coming from Spinningfield, one of the 'worst haunts of vice' in the city. He hurried off in the direction of the shouts and found a woman lying across the footpath and the doorway of a small house. A crowd of people had gathered around her and a flickering candle cast a dim light over the scene, giving the half-dressed woman 'a weird appearance'. The snow on the pavement was crimson with blood. The prone woman was a local character known as 'Fat Martha' and she had been stabbed.

Caminada drew out his rattle to summon help, which 'had the effect not only of summoning assistance but of bringing all the loose characters of the neighbourhood on the scene'. At the hideous noise, bedroom windows were flung open and heads leaned out of the upper windows of the neighbouring houses to find out what all the fuss was about. When the locals realised that it was only Martha they swore at the police officer for disturbing their sleep and slammed the windows shut again. There would be no help from that quarter.

Finally three other officers came to Caminada's assistance and he was dispatched to the police station for the accident litter, a handheld stretcher consisting of a piece of canvas stretched between two poles. As Martha weighed about 17 stone, the four men struggled to roll her onto the stretcher. Eventually they prised her from the cold pavement and headed towards the Royal Infirmary, followed by a procession of bedraggled onlookers. They made their unsteady way through the blizzard to the hospital, where they placed the victim on a couch in the accident ward for inspection by the surgeon on duty. When he discovered that Martha was a 'loose character', he refused to treat her and instructed the police officers to take her to the workhouse. Although 'the prospect for the carriers was not a pleasant one', they placed Martha back on the litter and set out again across the city for the workhouse hospital in New Bridge Street.

After nearly two miles of trudging through the snow with a dead weight, the exhausted foursome arrived at the workhouse gates and rang the bell. As the porter opened the heavy door, Martha stirred on the stretcher. 'Where am I?' she cried. Caminada replied that she was at the workhouse, to which she responded, 'What are you doing with me here? Put me down, you scoundrels. I am not going to the workhouse'. With these words she began to thrash, so the policemen were forced to put her back on the ground. Announcing that she was going home, she scrambled unsteadily to her feet and disappeared into the night. Caminada remarked:

the feelings of the carriers… can be better imagined than described, and… she was the recipient of some rather warm language, all of which she took in good part, and returned with interest… The incident was a common Deansgate one.

Despite his initial challenges on the beat, it did not take long for PC Caminada to get into his stride. By the end of his first year he had established himself as a resourceful and efficient police officer, who took the lead in operations. In December 1868, he was tasked with the investigation of the theft of a valuable collection of meerschaum pipes from a private house. The only information he had was a description of the suspect's 'striped, shining, cloth trousers'. After a week of searching Caminada finally found the suspect and his associates in a cellar dwelling in Peter Street. He organised an early morning raid on the lodgings, galvanising his colleagues into action: 'I set to work to call together all the constables near the point, giving them directions on each beat to be ready for a surprise, and to render me assistance if required'.

It was another bitterly cold night with hardened snow on the ground, and as they neared the dwelling Caminada removed his boots, overcoat and muffler, so that he would not be heard. He knew that one of the gang members, a prizefighter, would attack without hesitation if he spotted the police. Caminada watched the suspects through a shutter and noted that there was a deadly carving knife on the table. Placing two officers in a nearby street, he sent the rest into the alleyway: 'I now arranged for the lightest of the men to creep down the steps after me, and to leave his helmet at the top, for fear of it accidentally falling off'.

Masquerading as an associate of the gang, Caminada called through the door to the inhabitants. When they opened the door he rushed in, armed only with a staff and a bull's eye lantern, grabbing the knife from the table as he entered the dim room. Backed up by the other officers and with the knife in his hand, he handcuffed the gang. The prisoners were retained on remand while he tracked the movements of all the culprits, including 'shiny trousers Jack', who received nine months' penal servitude. The slick operation was a complete success.

During the early years of his police career, Caminada was credited with a number of high profile arrests, including a well-known group of 'base coiners' (forgers), the attempted robbery of a linen shop by convicted burglar, 'Oldham Johnny', and three seasoned criminals for burglary and arson, for which he was awarded £3 from the Salford Watch Committee. His success had enabled him to move out of the slums and he was now lodging at Albert Street Police Station, with 27 other constables, 20 prisoners and a homeless cotton-spinner. His mother and sister were living nearby in a shared house. Mary, 58, was working as a seamstress and Teresa, 23, as a silk binder in a local textile mill. Caminada's brother, John Baptiste, now aged 32, had moved to Nottingham, where he was working as a bookkeeper.

However, despite the improvement in Caminada's personal circumstances, life was about to become even tougher on the streets when he encountered ruthless career criminal, Bob Horridge. In 1869 complaints were coming into the Manchester Detective Office from errand boys whose parcels were being stolen. A man would approach the messengers and offer to deliver their consignments to spare them the journey. Unsurprisingly, the packages never reached their destination. One day, two errand boys caught the conman, and he turned out to be a close acquaintance of an ex-convict called Robert Horridge, who had been receiving the stolen parcels. PC Caminada called on Horridge at his home, accompanied by an inspector.

During the interview, Horridge became sullen and menacing. When he raised his scarred fists to threaten the policemen, Caminada took action: 'This led me to seize him and force him into a corner of the room, where I kept him until the search was completed'. Unable to find any evidence of the scam the officers left but, from that moment on, Caminada and Horridge became deadly rivals: 'We always knew each other afterwards, and whenever we met "Bob" would clench his teeth at me; but I always kept up a bold front to him, and never allowed him to think I was afraid of him'.

It was not long before Caminada had his chance to arrest Horridge, for the theft of a watch. On account of his previous 'bad character', Horridge was sentenced to seven years' penal servitude. Outraged by the severe sentence, he swore that on his release he would kill the policeman he considered responsible. During the next 20 years, Caminada and Horridge would come face-to-face many times, as the infamous thief continued to terrorise the streets of the city, with the detective always close on his tail. Horridge committed bold robberies, daring escapes and repeated assaults on police officers, including attempted murder.

Almost two decades later, the rivals would meet for the final time in a life-threatening confrontation, but in the meantime PC Caminada's career was on the rise.

Chapter Three

'Detective Jerome':
Racecourse Duty and Street Brawls
(1871–1876)

O n 2 March 1871, Police Constable Caminada was promoted to the rank of sergeant and, because 'he showed much aptitude for Detective work', he was transferred to the detective department. His professional ambition fulfilled, the newly appointed detective could now tackle crime in earnest.

The detective department of the Manchester City Police Force was in E Division and operated from the town hall, then located in King Street in the heart of the commercial district. However, plans were already under way for a new town hall that would dominate Manchester's developing cityscape. Designed by Alfred Waterhouse, the new Gothic-style building was opened in 1877, situated not far from where Caminada had lived as a boy. The police department occupied a suite of rooms in the back courtyard including an inquiry room, a rest room for officers on duty and six 13ft by 8ft cells, each one equipped with a water closet. The cobbled courtyard in the centre provided lighting and ventilation. It had a dipped pavement for the Black Marias to enter laden with prisoners. Detective Caminada would spend the rest of his career working in this building, eventually rising through the ranks to the position of detective superintendent.

Caminada was initially one of 23 detective sergeants. Every Friday at noon, they would all attend a parade at the town hall, where they would confer with the chief officer about ongoing inquiries. They were required to work 52 hours a week and had to submit regular reports of arrests, visits and cases. When he was promoted from police constable to detective sergeant, Caminada's salary would have almost doubled to around £2 per week. In addition, although the detectives' activities were mostly confined to crimes in their own division, their services could be hired out privately for special duty elsewhere in Manchester, (for 10s 6d a day) and outside the city (at a daily rate of £1 1s, plus expenses and third class travel). Detective

Caminada enthusiastically embraced this new opportunity and one of his first assignments away from home was at the Grand National in Aintree during 1871.

Horse-racing became increasingly popular throughout the nineteenth century and the racing season attracted huge numbers of people. As captured in William Powell Frith's famous painting, *Derby Day* (1856–58), all walks of life assembled at the racecourses to enjoy a day out. Well-heeled gentlemen rubbed shoulders with rural labourers wearing traditional smocks. Ladies in fine dresses indulged in picnics under lace parasols, while their children watched acrobats and tumblers perform tricks and gypsy women read fortunes nearby. All humanity was jostled together in the throng – politicians, aristocrats, factory workers and, of course, the criminal fraternity.

The most serious crime associated with racing was horse-stealing and even Sir Arthur Conan Doyle had Sherlock Holmes investigate a missing racehorse in 'Star Blaze' (*The Memoirs of Sherlock Holmes*, 1892). However, the most common offences were swindling and pickpocketing as racecourses, in Caminada's experience, were the ideal places to 'pluck greenhorns' (naïve newcomers): 'A racecourse is the centre of demoralisation to a neighbourhood for miles around and draws to it, as if by magnetic force, the scampdom of the country'.

The pickings were so rich that sharps, mobsmen and fake bookmakers flocked to the races to line their pockets. One of the most common tricksters was the 'thimble-rigger' who, with three small cups and a dried pea, outwitted day-trippers who laid bets that they could keep their eyes on the ball. Other gambling games included the three-card trick, loaded dice and weighted balls. Experienced magsmen were highly skilled and usually worked with an accomplice in the crowd to raise the stakes of the game. If spectators managed to keep hold of their money and resist the temptation of the side stalls, they could still lose it to a pickpocket.

The most agile thieves had no trouble slipping through the crowds at the races, lifting purses and watches, before disappearing again. These were no ordinary criminals, but were well-practised experts, who worked in teams. The gangs would select an appropriate victim and one of the mobsmen would come alongside him or her, as if squeezed by the crowd. While the victim's attention was focused on the race, the dipper would slip his fingers into a waistcoat or pocket and relieve the innocent spectator of his watch. Sometimes one pickpocket would distract the 'mark' by pushing into him, while an accomplice 'dipped' his pockets. As soon as the victim was successfully fleeced, the gang would simply melt away into the masses, their 'fences' waiting nearby to receive the stolen goods. These opportunistic crimes were so prevalent at race meetings that detectives would be sent from all over the country to watch over the unsuspecting public.

Before Detective Sergeant Caminada had even arrived at the racecourse at Aintree, he spotted two men whose appearance suggested that 'they followed no legitimate calling'. He decided to tail them and before long observed the tricksters in action. The pair entered a booth on the race-ground, where they stayed until the bell rang to clear the course. Caminada spotted them again, lurking near the grandstand, opposite the brick bars of the lower-class enclosure. This narrow space between the bars and the stand was one of the busiest of the ground and a great crowd had gathered there. One of the men positioned himself next to a punter, who was studying a race card that he was holding in both hands. The thief moved closer, clutching his own race card, until his elbows were touching those of the race-goer. His companion stood behind and slid his hands beneath the mark's elbows, lifting his gold watch from his breast pocket. Unfortunately, when the bell rang announcing the entrance of the horses, the detective lost his quarry in the ensuing rush. He was devastated: 'Here, on the first occasion when I was sent away from home on special duty, I had just been on the point of making an excellent capture and of earning the approval of my superiors, when all in a moment the opportunity was swept away'.

Undeterred, Caminada scrutinised the masses milling past him and was delighted to spot his two suspects once again. He watched from a distance as they slipped into a nearby field to disguise themselves. The detective lay down on the grass at a good vantage point from which to observe the thieves, who then bought some oranges from a woman hawking a basket on the edge of the field. When the bell for the next race rang, instead of going back to the racecourse they ran over to the railway station to meet their fence, unaware that Caminada was following close behind. As they handed over their booty, Caminada pounced, grabbing one man in each hand and dragging them into the station waiting room. Meanwhile, the fence jumped onto a departing train and made his escape. With no time to waste, Caminada called on the railway officials, 'in the name of the Queen', to assist him in the arrest, which they promptly did. Searching the suspects he found a gold watch, £36 in cash and a passage ticket to America. The men were convicted and sentenced to six months' imprisonment.

After that, Detective Caminada attended race meetings regularly and on another occasion at the Grand National, his disguise was so convincing that it even deceived his own chief constable. He had been detailed to take charge of the grandstand and while inspecting the ring he saw three men, dressed as 'swells', carrying out their customary tricks on an elderly gentleman with a walking stick. Caminada gave the signal for going undercover and he and his colleagues disguised themselves as labourers. Before long, the thieves tried to fleece another gentleman. One of the men, who was wearing glasses, put his hand on the victim's shoulder to steady himself, while he peered over the heads of the crowd, apparently looking for someone. His accomplice unbuttoned the man's overcoat with lightning speed and patted his pockets. This time they did not find anything, so they separated and moved on into the crowd near the grandstand.

Their next 'mark' was a gentleman who had carefully buttoned both his overcoat and undercoat, after placing his wallet in the inside pocket. The daring thief unbuttoned both coats, detached the chain from the man's watch, drew it out and passed it to his companion, who hurried off down the steps, where Caminada was lying in wait for him. The detective rounded up all three thieves and escorted them the short distance to the local police station, where he handcuffed them to a strapping officer.

Whilst this was going on, the Chief Constable rushed into the office, shouting that he had been robbed of his pocket watch. Forgetting that he was still in disguise, Caminada took out a watch that he had recovered from the thieves and showed it to his superior officer who, much to the amusement of everyone present, immediately began to interrogate him about its provenance. Caminada maintained his sangfroid as he explained the situation, but he could not resist the observation that even responsible police officers could sometimes become easy prey to thieves.

The development of the railways enabled criminals from all over Britain to travel to race meetings and, in order to remain one step ahead, detectives had to follow suit. On one such occasion Caminada was assigned to racecourse duty at the Goodwood Race Meeting, 'which, being a great rendezvous of fashion, attracts thieves from all parts of the kingdom'. The ever-vigilant detective started watching out for shady characters as soon as he changed trains at London. As he boarded the train at Victoria Railway Station, 'a stylishly-dressed man, carrying a macintosh across his arm' joined him. The fellow passenger engaged Caminada in a conversation about train times and offered him a cigar as they set off on their journey to Chichester. Sipping from a small flask of spirits, he regaled the undercover police officer with tales of fantastic bets he claimed to have won at the races.

As the train neared its destination, Caminada rushed into the corridor, accidentally leaving his travelling cape, hat, bag and umbrella on the overhead rack. In the crowds on the platform, he had spotted some familiar faces from home, including the pickpocket who had stolen the Chief Constable's watch at Aintree. As one of the thieves reached out to slip his hand into the pocket of a stranger standing on the platform, Caminada threw open the train door, jumped out of the moving train and seized the thieves, bundling them into a nearby lavatory. In the scuffle, the local police grabbed Caminada by mistake, while the other pickpockets, 'possessing better knowledge as to my identity, bolted in an instant'.

Once all the confusion had been sorted out and the prisoners apprehended, Caminada's travelling companion appeared with the belongings he had left behind in the compartment of the train. When the detective opened his bag and took out a pair of handcuffs, the man's jaw fell and he turned on his heel to flee the scene. The mysterious passenger was a London criminal, who went by the name of 'Red 'Un'. Even though he had slipped through Caminada's fingers, all was not lost. One of the men arrested on the platform, James 'Flying' Gibb, was a known felon convicted several times for theft, including once at the Old Trafford Steeplechases and, on another occasion, for stealing a tame rabbit. Each time Gibb had been sentenced to a short stretch in prison. On his release he had found legitimate employment too monotonous and soon 'blossomed into a very dangerous and expert thief', targeting jewellery shops in the city centre. Detective Caminada had arrested him for theft at least twice before, both times after a violent struggle.

When Caminada chanced upon Gibb at Chichester Railway Station, the thief was wanted for breaking his police supervision (now known as parole) back in Manchester. The detective took him before the local county magistrates, where the case against him was thrown out due to lack of evidence. The tenacious detective never arrested 'Flying Gibb' again. Gibb moved to London, where he became a 'continental thief', running his illegitimate business out of Charing Cross.

Detective Caminada visited widespread towns and cities in pursuit of felons. Just before Christmas in 1871, he received instructions to make enquiries about a gang of thieves, wanted in Sheffield for robbery with violence. One gang member had garrotted the victim whilst the others ransacked his pockets, and stole an expensive gold watch and chain. When Chief Superintendent Gee described one of the men as 'splay-footed' with very large feet, Caminada recognised him immediately as a criminal known as 'Footy'. He also identified his confederates as 'Cockney Johnny', Billy Boyd and Starkie. On learning that Cockney Johnny was in Leeds, he dashed over to the city on Christmas Eve.

On his arrival, Caminada traced the suspect to a house in York Street, a disreputable quarter of the city, where he recognised another member of the gang. John Roberts was a powerfully built man then wanted in London for murdering a known gambler, William Walsh, with a cavalry sword, after Roberts had had an affair with Walsh's wife. The detective could not believe his luck and, after summoning the assistance of local police officers, he staked out the house, spying on Roberts through one of the bedroom windows, as he sat at a dressing table. The officers arrested Roberts, who was then transferred to London and tried at the Old Bailey. With one case solved almost by accident, Caminada continued searching for Cockney Johnny. He slipped into disguise: 'I was made up in pretty good style to resemble more a denizen of the York Street district than a detective officer, and had my portrait been taken at the time I am quite sure that my friends would have failed to recognise me'.

It was 11pm on Christmas Eve and the streets were growing lively with late-night revellers, all full of festive cheer. Women stood on doorsteps with babies in their arms and young girls quarrelled over local men, some of whom were already drunkenly singing Christmas carols. Though still elated by his capture of Roberts, there would be no festivities for Caminada until he had caught his next prey. Standing in the shadows of the house where Johnny was purportedly living, he lit his pipe and waited. Before long a young woman passed him, whom he recognised as Johnny's companion, 'Yorkshire Charlotte'. Pretending to strike a match to light his pipe, Caminada asked the girl about Johnny and then whispered, 'Tell him "Billy" called'. He walked away from her, as he waited for his trick to work. Sure enough, a few minutes later, Cockney Johnny whistled to 'Billy' as a signal to enter the house. Still deep undercover, Caminada went in and greeted Johnny with an embrace, holding him tight until another officer came to his assistance. He then apprehended the astonished suspect, who failed to recognise his captor until he removed his disguise at the police station. Caminada bound himself to the prisoner, 'like Siamese twins', with a length of rope and transported him to Sheffield by train, arriving in the early hours of Christmas morning.

In the New Year, Sir William Henderson of the Metropolitan Police wrote to the Chief Constable of Manchester, commending Caminada for his part in the arrest of Roberts: 'The merit of the arrest of John Roberts is entirely due to him, and we fully appreciate his conduct on the occasion'. Detective Sergeant Caminada could not have received a better Christmas gift, even though Roberts was acquitted early the following year. It had been well worth working through the Christmas period and he probably had not missed any family festivities, as he was still lodging at the Albert Street Police Station.

Victorian police officers worked long hours and had little free time. They were required to be on duty during festivals and public holidays, which were usually rowdy occasions. Every year during Easter Week, the Knott Mill Fair was held in Deansgate. The main street was lined with stalls selling fragrant gingerbread and roasted chestnuts. Stallholders called out to young men to impress their sweethearts by having a go with a wooden mallet at the 'try your strength' machines or throwing a ring over a block to win a walking stick or knife. Children pestered their parents to let them try one of the countless lotteries or one-penny boards, in the hope of winning a cheap trinket. Millworkers and labourers chatted and drank beer, while ballad singers crooned and played barrel organs and accordions. For once, everyone was relaxed and carefree, with the exception of Detective Sergeant Jerome Caminada.

It was about 9.30pm and the detective was about to finish his shift for the day. He bade goodnight to a fellow officer and was walking along Deansgate through the busy stalls and lively crowds, when he saw two men shielding themselves from the light by the side window of a druggist's shop. Caminada slipped away from the blazing gas lamps into a darkened shop doorway to watch, as one man passed a small parcel to the other. His companion then walked over to a gingerbread stall and made a purchase. Shortly after, when an altercation broke out between the man and the stallholder, Caminada stepped in to arrest his suspects. As he conveyed them to Knott Mill Police Station, he noticed that one of the men was fiddling with his brace, which had come unfastened.

Later, when he searched the prisoners he found in the vest pocket of one a 'base' (fake) coin, with which the prisoner admitted that he had offered to buy the gingerbread. Well aware that passers of base coins worked in pairs, with one holding the 'swag' while the other, the 'smasher' or 'pitcher', used the coins one at a time to avoid detection, Caminada searched them again, but found nothing. Determined to prove his suspicions, he then began to strip them and found that the man with the faulty brace had a string attached to it, running down his trouser leg to a bag of coins wrapped in tissue paper at the bottom. He had been trying to release the bag when he was arrested, but the string had become knotted. Their ruse was up and they were both sentenced to five years' penal servitude. This was all in a night's work for Detective Caminada.

Within a few years of his promotion to the detective department, Caminada had become well-known within the criminal fraternity, who called him 'Detective Jerome' or 'Cammy', because of the difficulty of pronouncing his foreign surname. His encyclopaedic knowledge of the criminals lurking in the shadows of the city's underworld made him an exceptional detective. As Dr Watson observed of Sherlock Holmes in *A Study in Scarlet*, Caminada also regularly stalked the 'lowest portions of the City' after dark. However, some nights he was not alone in his nocturnal wanderings.

In the winter of 1874, a special correspondent for the *Manchester Evening News* undertook a covert study of the city's criminal underclass. Accompanied by an ex-convict, the reporter led his readers on a journey of discovery through the back alleys and closed courts of Manchester's most detestable streets, in order to show them, via a series of reports, what life was like for the 'outcasts and pariahs of the community'. One wet Saturday night in October, the journalist was exploring Deansgate with his 'guide', when they came across a fistfight between two women, who were tearing each other's hair out. A crowd of neighbours had gathered round and before long they began quarrelling amongst themselves. The argument soon descended into a free-for-all. As the reporter watched, a man appeared through the drizzle: 'it was soon put a stop to by… a man who I could see at once had more power over these unruly mobs than they would like to confess. He was of average build, but broadly set, and he "went for" the crowd instantly with a quiet determination'.

Without so much as a stick to protect himself, the stranger prised the two fighting women apart, thrusting one into the crowd and dragging the other into a nearby house. Then he returned to the onlookers, who were still arguing, and ordered them sharply to leave, calling each one by name, until they slid away into the darkness. One of the brawlers tried to stand his ground and called out menacingly, 'All right, you ___ Jerome', but, before he could say anymore, the man, who was of course Caminada, seized him by the collar, and ran him 'barrow-fashion' down the street. He shoved the man through his front door, before turning back to disperse the remaining stragglers, who slunk off back into the rookery. Within minutes calm was restored and the journalist was astounded that a single man could subdue a crowd of 'the lowest ruffians'. This unique eyewitness account revealed the famed detective in his element: fighting crime and restoring order to the streets of his city.

By the mid-1870s, Caminada had already established himself as an outstanding detective officer with considerable influence over the criminal fraternity, but his crime-busting work had still only just begun.

Chapter Four

Quack Doctors:
'Rascality, rapacity and roguery'
(1876–1877)

Urban life throughout Victorian England was precarious, but in Manchester it was downright deadly. Shoddy housing, inadequate water supplies and poor sanitation posed major health hazards for many city-dwellers, especially the most needy. As Alan Kidd states in *Manchester: A History*, the city's death rate between 1841 and 1851, was 33 per 1,000 inhabitants, second only to Liverpool, at 36. This was well above the national average of 22 per thousand in the first half of the nineteenth century. (In 2012, the mortality rate for the UK was 9.33.)

The death toll reached a peak in the late 1830s and mid–1840s, due to epidemics of typhus, influenza, diarrhoea and cholera. Engels noted in *The Condition of the Working Class in England in 1844*: 'That the dwellings of the workers in the worst portions of the cities, together with the other conditions of life of this class, engenders numerous diseases, is attested on all sides'.

Pulmonary tuberculosis was the main killer in Victorian Manchester and accounted for 10 per cent of all deaths. Contracted through infected droplets, the contagion spread like wild fire through the overcrowded tenements and poorly ventilated factories. Typhoid was even more lethal and passed easily through polluted water supplies, especially from standpipes in open cesspits and shared privies. Life in the slums was threatened further by outbreaks of cholera during each decade from 1830 to 1860. In *The Origin and Process of the Malignant Cholera in Manchester*, Dr Henry Gaulter recorded that of 1,325 people who contracted cholera in 1832, at least half died. In 1849, the killer disease claimed another 600 lives in the poorest quarters of the city. 'King Cholera' reigned without mercy.

Conditions in the factories and textile mills further aggravated the health of workers, toiling for long hours in the hot and dusty atmosphere of the workshops, alongside the constant deafening noise of the machines. The journalist Angus Bethune Reach, visited three cotton mills in Manchester in 1849 and was shocked at the sight of the unhealthy operatives:

The hue of the skin is the least favourable characteristic. It is a tallowy-yellow. The faces which surround you in a factory are, for the most part, lively in character, but cadaverous and overspread by a sort of unpleasant greasy pallor.

The contrast between the high temperatures on the factory floor and the damp, dank conditions in workers' homes meant that many suffered from permanent colds and afflictions of the lungs, such as asthma, bronchitis and pneumonia. Prolonged periods of time spent operating machines performing repetitive movements in the same position, left many with physical deformities that affected their hips, backs and limbs. They suffered swollen joints, varicose veins and ulcers on their calves and thighs. Lack of sleep, due to the unremitting factory hours, exacerbated their problems, leading to indigestion, irritation of the nervous system and general weakness.

In his 1833 report, *The Manufacturing Population of England*, Peter Gaskell gave a graphic description of cotton mill workers:

Their complexion is sallow and pallid, with a peculiar flatness of feature… Their stature low – the average height… being five feet six inches. Their limbs slender, and playing badly and ungracefully. A very general bowing of the legs. Great numbers of girls and women walking lamely or awkwardly, with raised chests and spinal flexures. Nearly all have flat feet.

Children suffered even more than adults; most starting work in the mills from the tender age of five or six. They faced not only stunted growth and illness, but also the ever-present threat of accidents, as they slipped under the machines to pull a stray thread from the whirring spools.

At the more fortunate end of the social scale, (as outlined in the *Report on the Sanitary Condition of the Labouring Population of Great Britain* compiled by Edwin Chadwick in 1844), the average life expectancy of 'professional persons and gentry, and their families' in Manchester in 1842 was 38 years, two decades more than the 18 years expected among the working classes. This formed a striking contrast, even though the latter would have been skewed by the high infant mortality rate. Chadwick also commented: 'It is an appalling fact that, of all who are born in the labouring districts of Manchester, more than 57 per cent die before they attain 5 years of age, that is, before they can be engaged in factory labour'.

It is not surprising that the wealthy moved out of the city to the more salubrious suburbs, hoping to increase their chances of good health and a longer life. Statistics like these reveal the real risk of illness and the likelihood for most of an early death. This led to an all-consuming preoccupation with health amongst the citizens of Victorian Manchester, whatever their social status.

Detective Sergeant Caminada discovered this phenomenon by chance in 1876. It was a Saturday evening and Caminada was making his way home after a hard day's work at the detective office, when he passed a pawnbroker's shop on Deansgate. As he walked by, Caminada saw the manager, who was a friend of his, and popped in for a quick gossip. Inside the shop, the pawnbroker and his assistant were perusing some prints laid out on the counter and, on the other side, there was a young man 'whose appearance was striking in the extreme'. He left a strong impression on Caminada:

His cheeks were hollow, shrivelled, and cadaverous; his eyes large and unnaturally bright; his form shrunken and bent; and altogether he had the appearance of one to whom life was a burden, and to whom a natural death would be a happy release.

Suspicious of the provenance of the prints and alarmed by the client's countenance, Caminada questioned him and ascertained that the prints had been stolen from the man's employer. After arresting him, the detective proceeded to search his house and was shocked at what he found there: 'in two tin trunks I discovered one hundred and fifty-three doctor's bottles, eighty-six of which either did contain or had contained medicine, and the rest had been used for lotions'.

The thief had fallen into the grip of a ruthless quack doctor and when Caminada interrogated him further, the whole sorry tale was revealed: 'he then made a clean breast of as foul a piece of rascality, rapacity, and roguery as I ever met with'. The young man had received a pamphlet in the street and after reading it, he became convinced that he was 'hopelessly afflicted with all the horrible ailments most graphically set forth in that insidious and diabolical pamphlet'. His only hope, he believed, was to seek the 'miraculous curative powers' of the doctor who had issued the material.

But the 'medicine' had had the opposite effect and gradually his health had deteriorated. Meanwhile, he was rapidly spending his savings to procure more potions and once he had run out of money, the 'doctor' suggested a loan company, which ultimately led to his descent into crime. Inspired by this pitiful story, Caminada decided to put an end to the nefarious practices of the fake doctors, who callously exploited the weak and vulnerable. Referring to them as 'bloodsuckers of the human race', he considered them to be one of the worst kinds of criminal: 'Quacks are, in truth, greater enemies to society than the garotter or the burglar'. What particularly irked Caminada was that their chief victims were the poor and, convinced that these 'doctors' were completely fraudulent, he determined to expose them.

In the nineteenth century, the trade of quack doctors flourished in Manchester. Intelligent and expert con artists, they knew how to exploit the fears of a public strongly aware of their imminent mortality. Caminada soon found that many of them lived in 'large and handsomely furnished houses, and dressed in the height of fashion, sporting splendid jewellery'. They set up practices in plush office suites complete with waiting rooms, surgeries and medical equipment. Their advertisements and pamphlets flooded the city, enticing passersby with cures and tonics for all manner of illnesses. They organised special consultations in public venues, where potential patients could discuss their health problems for free.

Once the victims had unburdened themselves of their anxieties, they would be offered a miraculous cure to restore their health – but this time, it would require a fee. The relentless cycle began with the patient needing more medicine, which the doctor would supply at an exorbitant cost. As their funds dwindled and their fear of death increased, the doctors would offer the services of a loan company so that the patient could continue their 'treatment'. With no one to regulate these counterfeit medical practices, the victim soon descended into debt or a life of petty crime, as they endeavoured to keep up with the payments in a desperate effort to preserve their fragile health. Caminada outlined the modus operandi of these 'pitiless harpies' in his memoirs:

When the disease is hopeless, and medical men abandon the patient, the quack takes him in hand, and gives him an impetus towards the grave, while at the same time he rifles his pockets. The very essence of the system is to exhaust the physical powers to such a degree that the nostrums produce no effect unless they are taken in constantly increasing potions.

On 24 October 1876, Caminada visited a 'Dr Lewis' at his premises. When the undercover detective told him that he had been experiencing a pain in his heart and was troubled by 'sweaty' hands, the doctor offered to treat him at a cost of 10s 6d and asked him to return the following day with a urine sample. Caminada went straight to a local chemist's and bought a mixture comprising six ounces of water, three drops of hydrosulphide of ammonia and 10 drops of saffron syrup. When he returned to Dr Lewis's house, the doctor examined him and listened to his chest with a stethoscope, before pronouncing his diagnosis: 'You are suffering from extreme nervousness, but your heart is all right. I have some medicine that will act on the blood and nerves at once'. With that, he produced a potion that Caminada was to take for three weeks at a cost of 40 guineas (roughly £3,000 today). When Caminada asked him for the results of his urine sample, he shook his head saying it was 'very bad'.

The detective returned to the surgery five days later with a warrant for Dr Lewis's arrest. In the meantime, the city analyst had tested the 'medicine' and found it to be a compound of tincture of cardamom and sal volatile (an early form of baking powder), often prescribed for weakness and faintness in the form of a warm cordial drink. Doctor Lewis was arrested and fined £20. The same week Caminada brought 12 other charlatan doctors to trial.

One of them was Charles Davies Henry, whom the detective had visited at his place of business while disguised as a warehouse worker, and again claming to be suffering from a pain in his heart and sweating hands. The doctor examined his tongue, felt the muscles of his arms and took his pulse, before concluding that his state was 'a most deplorable one' and that he was 'in a sad condition of despondency'. He prescribed some medicine and gave the patient general advice on how to improve his health, which included washing in cold water every morning, taking exercise with dumb-bells, having a glass of bitter beer with dinner and drinking only one cup of tea a day, and never green tea. He also exhorted Caminada to have plenty of company, to go to the theatre and to ride outside omnibuses.

When this information was later relayed in court, the public gallery burst into laughter. The doctor prescribed a 'thorough course of treatment' costing £10, which he offered to accept in instalments. Analysis revealed that the medicine was simple iron salts. Henry was fined £15.

Caminada was commended for his actions against the phony doctors in the *Manchester Courier*:

> *The subject is an unpleasant one in every sense; but the evil wrought to society by these rapacious impostors is so enormous that we should certainly not be doing our duty did we not seek to enforce the plain lesson taught by the relation of Sergeant Caminada's adventures.*

Following his initial success, Caminada went on to expose many more quack doctors. In one case he received instructions to investigate a complaint about a pamphlet, advertising a miracle cure called 'A Grain of Gold'. Through information gained from a clerk employed to stick gummed labels on the leaflets, Caminada discovered the likely identity of the author.

One evening, carrying a black bag, a travelling rug and a walking stick, Caminada went to the surgery at Acton House, in Bridge Street near the Queen's Theatre. An elderly man opened the door and ushered the detective into an elegantly furnished apartment, with long curtains hanging from the ceiling. After a few moments, a professional-looking gentleman wearing a long cloak entered the room and asked him to explain his symptoms. Presenting himself as a clerk for a firm of solicitors in Buxton, Caminada outlined his imaginary illness. The doctor examined his tongue and felt his pulse. He declared that Caminada was 'in a very bad way', but he could cure him within three weeks at a cost of £10. The crook doctor was Arthur Chadwick, alias Buchanan. He had started his career as a tailor's apprentice but had been arrested for theft. After that, he went through a number of questionable occupations, before finally re-inventing himself as 'an eminent specialist'.

One of Chadwick's colleagues in crime was Dr Nelson, who held his practice in the upmarket area of King Street. Caminada sent two officers to the black and gold-painted premises, easily identified by a plaque on the door with 'Medical Institute' emblazoned in gilt letters. There were window boxes on the sills and a large lamp of coloured glass hanging over the entrance. Once again the chambers were ornately furnished, with oil paintings in gilt frames and statues on pedestals. One officer was disguised as a butcher from Bakewell and the other as a factory worker from Accrington. They were both diagnosed as suffering from consumption. Nelson, whose real name was William Kay, was originally a weighing clerk at a colliery in Derbyshire, before rising through the ranks of the sham medical profession to become a partner in the 'Medical Institute'. Chadwick was later sentenced to 18 months' imprisonment with hard labour and Kay, six months. After the trial, Caminada secured the money in Chadwick's bank account and used it to repay those he had swindled.

Despite his skill at disguise and his considerable success in bringing many bogus doctors to justice, Detective Caminada would meet one very accomplished swindler, who would prove to be more than his match. In 1877 Caminada spotted an advertisement for the 'Food of Foods', a medicine sold by the Reverend E. J. Silverton of Nottingham. The tonic had apparently performed miracles for a variety of ailments and was particularly effective in curing deafness. Immediately distrustful, Caminada wrote to the reverend, pretending he was the superintendent of a Sunday school and keen to get married but currently in the grip of a mysterious illness. By return of post, he received further testimonials of Silverton's miraculous cures and a questionnaire, as well as a request for an advance fee of 27s 6d.

In Nottingham the Reverend Edward James Silverton was a well-known and highly respected Baptist Minister, who had funded a new church for his congregation. When the Mayor of Nottingham had opened Exeter Hall in 1876, the *Nottinghamshire Guardian* had reported, 'There was something noble in the venture of their pastor, Mr Silverton, who must have great confidence in the sentiment of the human heart'. This statement would later prove to be prophetic, but in a more sinister way. The mayor had presented Silverton with a decorated scroll, conveying the congregation's 'great esteem and affection'.

Caminada continued the correspondence, before handing the matter over to an interested society to investigate further, whose activities resulted in the reverend moving his headquarters to London. Yet, when Silverton's advertisements began to reappear on billboards in Manchester, Caminada decided that it was time to meet this famous doctor. Silverton had obviously been doing well and on this visit he hired the Free Trade Hall, where he delivered a series of health lectures and offered free daily consultations. Caminada pretended to be suffering from gout and, putting on an old shoe, he limped into the hall.

Reverend Silverton was not available, so he saw his assistant who, without examining Caminada's foot, diagnosed rheumatism and advised 'a good clearing out' at a charge of 35 shillings, which was at least double the average worker's weekly wage. The detective followed the advice and purchased the proffered 'Food of Foods' tonic. On leaving the hall, he finally met Silverton, an intelligent-looking man with bushy sideburns and small, round-rimmed glasses, who offered him a follow-up consultation.

On analysis the miraculous 'Food of Foods' was found to be nothing more than lentils, bran, brown flour and water. The 'Elixir of all Diseases' was definitely a scam. Caminada obtained summonses against Silverton and his assistant, surgeon Charles Mitcheson, for conspiracy to defraud. The publicity encouraged many individuals to come forward to share their stories of extortionate fees and merciless exploitation by these duplicitous doctors. One particularly distressing case was that of a poor woman, who had even sold her bed to gain medical advice for her ailing son. Nevertheless,

Caminada's investigation did not end quite as he had hoped, as neither the Medico-Ethical Society nor the public prosecutor would take up the case. The stipendiary magistrate offered to bind Caminada over to prosecute Silverton at his own cost but he declined, hoping that the adverse publicity would be sufficient to put the charlatan out of business once and for all.

Unfortunately, this clever impostor remained at large and continued practising medicine with his daughter, who later joined his flourishing business. When he spotted an advertisement for her services on a special visit to Manchester in the newspapers, Caminada sent a detective to her surgery disguised as a 'deaf' cattle dealer. He also wore blue spectacles to give the impression that he had a problem with his eyes. The female 'doctor' gravely informed the 'cattle dealer' that he was indeed afflicted with deafness and would lose his hearing altogether without treatment. She added that his hearing problems were also affecting his sight.

After this, Caminada could not resist an opportunity to see this 'lady quack' for himself, so he went to her surgery on the second floor of the Mosley Hotel. When his turn came, a stylishly dressed woman ushered him into the office where, in the centre of the room, there was a table covered with ear trumpets. The female doctor, also wearing fashionable clothes, asked him about his complaint in 'the most silvery tones'. She then took a small lamp and placed a tube in Caminada's ear. After the examination, she said that the hearing in his right ear was partly destroyed and entirely gone in the other, for which she proposed a four-month course of treatment at a cost of £29 6d. Caminada concluded that Miss Silverton was just as much a fraud as her father: 'This lady quack, a worthy descendant of her "wonderful-curing" papa, had not been tutored in vain'.

The Reverend E. J. Silverton continued his dishonest practice with no further challenges until his death in 1895, at the age of 60. At his well-attended funeral another local clergyman, the Reverend Joseph Clark gave a moving eulogy, as reported in the *Nottingham Evening Post*:

We feel as we commit the precious dust of our departed friend to his grave that we are committing one who was a loving husband, an indulgent father, and a true friend, whose tongue was eloquent for Christ, and whose heart beat true in the cause of his fellow men.

Had Caminada been in attendance, he would have added his own searing tribute to this con artist, who exploited hapless victims with his 'eloquent tongue' and defied the law for 30 years.

Despite his repeated attempts, Caminada was unable to rid the streets completely of dubious medical practitioners:

Quack doctors have unfortunately infested society for many generations. Although many attempts have been made to expose them, yet they have, by means of fraudulent pretences and almost fabulous sums spent in advertising, carried on a lucrative business in all parts of the kingdom.

As social conditions improved towards the end of the century, there was less need for their disreputable ministrations. However, there were plenty of other clever charlatans with elaborate ruses waiting to take their place, as well as an endless supply of gullible targets.

Chapter Five

Sophisticated Swindles and Cunning Confidence Tricks
(1878–1884)

Few cities in the world have within them so many thieves as Manchester. The pavement of Cottonopolis is incessantly trodden by rogues. This is not surprising. The facility afforded for hiding in a crowd induces those who are badly disposed to resort hither from all parts of the globe. A great number of these persons are fixed constantly in this great City. Some come only like birds of passage – at the approach of great occasions, or during the racing or other busy seasons. Among those permanently located in the City are a class of thieves of incredible effrontery, who work what is called the "confidence trick".

(Jerome Caminada, *Twenty-Five Years of Detective Life, 1895*)

With his unerring instinct for rooting out deception, Caminada tackled all kinds of con artists and swindlers. He solved numerous cases involving a colourful cast of shady characters, who used aliases and nicknames to evade arrest. Some operated simple confidence tricks, like 'ringing the changes' and the 'ring dropping' scam, while others ran complex and often seemingly impenetrable ruses.

In 1878 a deputation from the Manchester and Salford Association of Pawnbrokers lodged a complaint about a rise in the pledging of fake, or 'duff', jewellery. The chief constable handed the matter over to Caminada. After making enquiries, he discovered that the racketeers placed advertisements in the local newspapers for loans, in return for pawn tickets for valuable articles as security. When potential moneylenders redeemed the tickets they would find that the pawned jewellery was worth far less than the money they had naïvely handed over. By responding to the requests, Caminada gathered enough evidence to arrest the gang of six men who perpetrated the 'deep-laid conspiracy'.

The ringleader was known as 'Diamond Sam', because he never missed an opportunity to sell sham jewellery. There was also 'Crack Shot', who happened to share his surname with a winner of the Elcho Challenge Shield, a shooting competition run by the National Rifle Association: a feat of which he used to boast vicariously. Another gang member was known as 'Little Ted', or the 'Take Down', due to his ability as a salesman. After Caminada took them into custody, more witnesses came forward and it transpired that, as well as jewellery, dummy pledges included tickets for furniture, a piano and even a cask of cognac. Diamond Sam was sentenced to five years' penal servitude, Crack Shot to 18 months and the Take Down was discharged, due to a technical error in the indictment.

Many classic Victorian confidence tricks were strikingly simple and practised magsmen, like Diamond Sam and his mates, expertly operated charades to deceive their prey. Most began at country fairs and racecourses where they ran gambling games, such as thimble rigging and cards, then progressed to the cities, where they developed more elaborate ruses, such as 'ringing the changes', a widely practised trick, also used to dispose of counterfeit coins. Caminada knew this con well: 'This is a class of theft which differs from all others, in that it requires a good deal of boldness and self-possession'.

The dodge began with two people entering a shop or public house. One would place an order and then tender a sovereign in payment. As soon as he received the change, his companion would say that he had a coin of a smaller denomination, and offer to pay. He would then hand over a half-sovereign to the salesperson, who returned the first coin and gave change for the second, but without recovering the change given for the first sovereign. The object was to confuse or 'bustle' the sales assistant and if they succeeded, the thieves would receive the change for each coin offered. By the time the person serving realised what was happening, the sharps would have already disappeared.

In 1884 two men plagued Manchester businesses, by running this type of fraud. One was 'a very easy-going fellow, a slow talker' and the other, 'a man of gentleman-like appearance who, in almost every case, produced from his coat pocket patterns of cloth at which his companion looked'. Caminada set out to find these mysterious strangers. He was walking along City Road, when he came across one of them and arrested him. At the detective office, the suspect claimed that it was a case of mistaken identity, but when Caminada found the pattern books in his pocket, there was no doubt that he had the right man. Caminada then arrested his accomplice, with the help of a tramcar driver who had spotted him in Stretford. Both were tried and sentenced to nine months' imprisonment.

Detective Caminada investigated another classic con during the same year. This common deceit would focus on a stranger in town and relied on building trust between the sharper and the target, usually in the convivial atmosphere of a public house. In one case, a farmer was returning from the market in central Manchester, when a stranger stopped him to ask about train times. After a brief discussion, the man invited the farmer for a drink in a nearby tavern, where a second man joined them. During the conversation the farmer mentioned that he was from Cheshire, at which point the newcomer announced that coincidentally his father had died recently, leaving £400 to be distributed among the poor of Cheshire. He then suggested sharing the amount between the farmer and his new acquaintance for them to distribute, each receiving a payment of £20 for their trouble. The only condition was that they provide securities for the amount. Both men accepted, and arranged to meet the following day with the appropriate funds.

The next day, as agreed, the farmer produced two Bank of England hundred pound notes, which he had been hiding in his chimney for fear of banks and thieves. While the benefactor was holding the envelope containing the cash, he took off his hat to wipe his brow, surreptitiously swapping the bank notes for pages of *Bradshaw's Railway Guide*. By the time the farmer realised, the two sharpers had jumped into a passing hansom cab and fled. A few minutes later, they cashed one of the notes at the Bank of England.

The police circulated a description of one of the 'strangers': he had a dark complexion, wore a long beard and was dressed in a dark tweed coat, grey trousers and a silk hat. He had signed his name as 'Henry Johnson' on the back of the note. Detective Caminada recognised Johnson as a man he had previously arrested for the 'ringing the changes' scam. When he compared the signature on the bank note with the relevant entry in the police book, his suspicions were confirmed. Next he traced some of the changed notes to a London tradesman, where Johnson had purchased some clothes. The bank tracked the second £100 note to a café in Boulogne, which was run by a well-known 'fence' and frequented by English and French railway and steamboat thieves. All that remained now was to capture the crook.

One evening when Caminada was passing the Old Fleece Inn, a well-known haunt of thieves near Smithfield market in Manchester, a fight broke out. To Caminada's surprise, Johnson ran straight past him. The detective immediately gave chase and, despite receiving a violent blow, he seized the felon and dragged him into a nearby cheesemaker's shop to wait for assistance. Due to Caminada's quick thinking, Johnson was later sentenced to 10 years' penal servitude.

In addition to more straightforward confidence tricks, Detective Caminada was also responsible for exposing some highly sophisticated scams which had claimed many victims. The operators of these elaborate, but fake, businesses and schemes were usually educated individuals who appeared to be 'swells'; they were well-dressed, articulate and, above all, utterly convincing. Later, Caminada warned readers of his memoirs about their allure:

> *The swindler is invariably well practised in the art of shuffling, and as a rule is a very agreeable and pleasant character. He has a smiling, cheerful manner which is quite captivating. But beware of him. He is a cunning fellow, and will probably give you a world of trouble before you have done with him.*

One such criminal was Alfred Oram, a solicitor, whom Caminada encountered twice in connection with complicated scams. The first time was in 1879, when Oram collaborated in a jewellery racket with another crook, Thomas Kavanagh, who was eventually convicted at the Old Bailey for conspiracy to defraud. Oram escaped the law that time but, as with Johnson, Caminada would remember him and eventually run him to ground.

The investigation began when the detective received a complaint from local residents of loud noises at night coming from a tobacconist's in Chorlton Road, Hulme. Caminada called at the shop to buy some cigars and found that the young woman in charge was keen to help with his enquiries, so he arranged to meet her after her shift. In the company of a female officer, he had tea with the shop assistant and learned that her employers often came to the shop after dark. On the promise of 'something handsome for her trouble', the woman gave him the shop keys and, that evening, Caminada gained access through the outer door and then used a picklock to enter the inner rooms. One of the rooms had counters fitted with mock drawers, and the shelves held empty cigar boxes. In another he found a large empty wooden case, as well as framed oleographs, a portmanteau of old clothes and a large quantity of wood shavings. From experience he knew that he had found the preparations for arson and that the shop was likely to be heavily insured.

Stationing his officers in a house opposite, Caminada maintained a close watch on the premises. At dusk one Sunday evening, his colleagues reported that two men had entered the tobacconist's in suspicious circumstances. The detective took up their positions and when one of the men left the shop to stand outside on the pavement under a gas lamp, he recognised him as the solicitor, Oram. The other man joined him and the officers tailed the pair across town to Broughton, before losing them.

Sure enough, the following Saturday Caminada gained information of a fire at the tobacconist's. By the time he arrived, the fire brigade had extinguished the flames, but during his inspection of the premises, he noticed that a number of meerschaum pipes, cigar-holders and the oleograph prints were missing. Furthermore, he found that the gas-fittings had been cut in several places. Two pipes had been laid from the original plumbing, but without burners or taps, and a piece of string tied to the handle so that the gas could be turned on from outside the building. There was also evidence that phosphorous had been planted inside the shop to encourage the flames.

During the investigation, a man came into the shop to take possession of the premises. On questioning him, Caminada obtained a note from the man's employer, who was none other than Oram, with the address of his business. When he arrived at the office, he found the solicitor at his desk, with a copy of *Medical Jurisprudence* by Alfred Swaine Taylor open at the page on combustible materials. After a brief fight, Caminada arrested Oram and, while he was detained at the detective office, Caminada searched his house, where he found the missing items from the tobacconist's, including the oleographs. Alfred Oram was sentenced to 10 years' penal servitude.

Another complex trick was the 'long firm fraud', which Caminada explained as: 'principally carried on by experienced swindlers, who work into each others' hands, and whilst at times very difficult to track they cause great loss to the mercantile community'. The first stage in the operation was to rent an office or warehouse in the business quarter of a city. Then, using headed stationery and formal business cards, the 'proprietor' would send out orders for equipment and furnishings, which would subsequently be sold or auctioned. When the creditors came to demand payment, the 'business' would have vanished.

In 1880 a businessman hired a warehouse in Aytoun Street, close to the city centre. Describing himself as a 'general merchant', he furnished his new office with carpets, silks and prints, as well as the requisite office supplies. After having sent for samples, he then placed orders for goods, paying in cash for small items in order to create confidence, before placing much larger orders. In this way, the thief acquired goods amounting to thousands of pounds, which he and his accomplices pawned or sold. The victims of the conspiracy and their solicitors enlisted Caminada's help in tracing the culprits. Following a tip-off from a salesman, the detective travelled to Liverpool with his informant to track them down. While they were in an omnibus by the docks, his companion recognised a gentleman carrying a black bag as one of the men they were searching for. Caminada jumped off the 'bus and arrested him. At a local police station, he found jewellery that the crook had exchanged for goods in the suspect's bag, as well as a business card with his associate's address in London.

The owner of a carpet firm paid Caminada's expenses of £20 to travel to London to complete his investigation. The detective went straight to the address in Islington, asked for the man in question and, on gaining entry, rushed up the stairs to the bedroom with a warrant for his arrest. The suspect seized a razor, intending to commit suicide, but Caminada flew at him and, after a struggle, gained possession of the improvised weapon. He then transported the prisoner back to Manchester to stand trial with his partner in crime. They received sentences of seven and five years' imprisonment.

In Detective Caminada's experience, the very worst kinds of swindlers were those who played on the vulnerability of the poor. In the course of his career, he encountered many bogus charities and societies, including an emigration agency, a registry office, and even a fake ragged school. One of the most widely reported scandals was the Next-of-Kin fraud, which Caminada exposed in 1882.

One morning in May 1882, the detective was walking through the city centre, when a police officer stopped him to ask for assistance: a gentleman named Barkley had made a complaint about being cheated out of some money. Whilst the three of them were discussing the matter, Barkley spotted the alleged swindler crossing the road. Caminada took up the trail, shadowing him to the headquarters of the 'International Law Agency', further along Market Street. Inside the office several people were waiting to enter an inner room, where the manager, Arthur McKenzie, was dealing with requests. Caminada burst straight in and asked McKenzie about his employer. He replied that the proprietor was an attorney by the name of Rogers, before ordering the detective to leave the office at once. Caminada stood his ground and proceeded to take the statement of Barkley, who had made the original complaint.

Two years earlier, Mr Barkley had seen an advertisement in the *Manchester Evening News* about claiming property as next-of-kin. As his father had been making a claim to an estate for some years, Barkley had applied to the

International Law Agency on his behalf, for help with the petition. Rogers had agreed to take on the suit, following payment of an initial fee of £1 12s 6d (about £134 today) and 10 per cent commission thereafter, on any property recovered. Once the papers had been presented, Rogers stated that the case was more complicated than he had realised and in order to proceed, he would need to incur further costs. This was the standard practice for the agency; the costs would escalate and the hapless 'heir' would have no choice but to keep on paying, in the hope that they would be recompensed, once they had inherited their estate.

Barkley paid a further £32 6d and was delighted to receive the news that his father had been granted a judgment in his favour. Rogers arranged to travel with them, at their expense, to Market Drayton to take possession of one of the farms on the estate. The house was empty, but on Rogers's instructions, the father and son entered the property and locked the door behind them. Shortly afterwards two police constables arrived, accompanied by a crowd of locals armed with pitchforks, and the pair were arrested. Rogers was nowhere to be seen.

While Mr Barkley was relating his story, another 50 people in the office beset Detective Caminada, each with their own sorry tale. Many had arrived with bags and satchels, ready to transport their inherited funds away, but they now realised that they had fallen into a trap. Caminada arrested McKenzie and on searching the premises he found 270 bundles of wills, plans of estates, family trees, engraved plates, letter headings and correspondence. He then set about investigating the complaints of many other people who had been conned by this ruthless gang. One especially heartless case involved three elderly women who had sold their furniture to obtain a loan of £15, which they were paying back at a rate of five shillings per week; all to pursue their supposed inheritance of £9,000.

McKenzie's fellow conspirators were soon apprehended. James Stodden Rogers had established the International Law Agency and represented himself as a Crown solicitor, who was able to recover money from Chancery. He was joined in business by John Henry Shakespeare, a bona fide solicitor, and two others. Before long they had opened offices in Manchester, Birmingham, Glasgow and London. They advertised their services in the newspapers and even published a pamphlet, *Authentic Lists of Heirs*, which comprised a list of potential inheritors. Once the subject had taken the bait, the swindlers went to considerable lengths to keep them hooked.

A widow from Manchester, Elizabeth Roach, visited the agency after seeing a name on the list that was very similar to her own. The estate, part of which had been apparently bought by the Midland Railway Company for the construction of St Pancras Station, was valued at £20,000. She paid £32 6d to initiate proceedings and McKenzie invited her to London, at her own expense, to oversee the application. Her experiences were reported in the *Nottingham Evening Post*: 'They took her to a place called Somerset House, where she saw a person described as a judge, sitting at a table, with a wig and gown on'. The process turned out to be more protracted than anticipated, so there were more documents to sign and pay for back in Manchester, as well as two further trips to London. During one visit to the capital, she was required to sign a large parchment but, as she was illiterate, she even ended up paying £1 17s 6d for them to show her how to write her name.

When claimants ran out of funds the agency would offer to issue bonds as security to enable them to borrow from friends and family, who expected a return on their investment after the acquisition of the estate. This happened in the case of Mrs Roach, as she paid costs of around £200, that she could ill afford. The scammers repeated this deception with great success, the claims becoming more convoluted and the costs escalating. Detective Caminada travelled to London to find out how the ruse worked. He discovered that the sharps left their clients in the public gallery of the court while they spoke to the clerk, thus reassuring them that their petition was legitimate. Next the dupes were taken to Somerset House, where anyone could look at a will for one shilling. They then proceeded to Somerset Chambers next door, where they swore on an affidavit before a commissioner for the administration of oaths.

Most of the cases were aborted on the arrest of the organisers, who were found guilty of having conspired by 'divers false pretences and subtle devices' to obtain money, with the intent to cheat and defraud. Rogers was sentenced to two years' hard labour and his confederates received 12 months each. Shakespeare died two months into his sentence. Five years after his release, McKenzie was convicted again at the Old Bailey to 10 years' penal servitude for a further series of frauds. The money handed over by the unfortunate victims of the International Law Agency was never recovered and, despite his endeavours to help them, not everyone appreciated Caminada's assistance. At least one gentleman believed that he would have acquired his estate, were it not for the interference of the meddling detective.

Caminada's considerable skill in unravelling these intricate scams and his indefatigable detective work led to two promotions. On 6 April 1882, he was made Inspector and then, just two years later, on 12 June 1884, he was promoted to chief inspector. This rapid ascent in his career was mirrored in his personal life. By 1881, Caminada was lodging with a police constable and his wife in the more upmarket district of Chorlton-on-Medlock, where his neighbours were mainly manufacturers and clerks. On 19 December 1881 he got married, but the rest of the decade would see difficult times for the newly-wed couple. Soon the very thieves and con artists whom he spent his days apprehending would strike at the heart of his own family.

Chapter Six

'Even my own fireside':
Trouble at Home
(1884)

On a cold, showery morning, a week before Christmas 1881, Jerome Caminada married Amelia Wainhouse in the Roman Catholic Church of the Holy Name of Jesus, Manchester. The church had been built on Oxford Road only a decade before, designed by Joseph Hansom, famous for the 'Patent Safety Cabs' that still bear his name. The detective, aged 37, made his vows to his bride, who was 10 years his junior, in a simple ceremony witnessed by Amelia's older brother, Thomas, and her sister, Sarah Anne.

Amelia was the daughter of Joseph Wainhouse, an Irish ribbon weaver, and his wife, Mary. Like the Caminadas, the family came from humble beginnings in the mill-dominated suburb of Hulme, depicted by Engels as 'one great working people's district'. Due to the steep rise in the population following the Industrial Revolution, it was an area of tiny back-to-back houses, inadequate sanitation and dreadful conditions. Born in 1855, Amelia had three older siblings: Thomas, William and Sarah Anne, and a younger brother, Joseph. Unlike Caminada's family, all the Wainhouse children survived childhood and they quickly left the slums behind. At the time of her wedding, Amelia was living with her brother Thomas and his wife, Annie. Aged 31, Thomas was a successful chemical salesman and Annie was an organist and music teacher. Amelia's other brothers also shared the house, along with their mother Mary, 58, now a widow. William, 28, was a pattern maker for an engineer and Joseph, 22, a lithographic printer. Amelia was also working, as a saleswoman, probably with Thomas.

Further proof of the Wainhouse family's success was the fact that they had moved to Moss Side. In the mid-nineteenth century Moss Side was still a quiet, picturesque village on the outskirts of Manchester. Between 1861 and 1901, the population of this sleepy suburban backwater increased tenfold to 27,000, as it was subsumed into the urban conglomeration. In the early 1880s, although they lived in a street of small terraced houses, the Wainhouses would have enjoyed a relatively pleasant lifestyle in a mixed area, which also included large, middle class houses, with notable residents such as Rupert Potter, father of children's author Beatrix. Friedrich Engels took shelter in Moss Side after his travels around the unsanitary inner city. Close to Alexandra Park, with many fine buildings like the Denmark Hotel, it was a far cry from Amelia's birthplace in the slums still home to most of the Caminadas.

Jerome and his new wife set up home in Old Trafford, another leafy suburb closer to the city centre. They bought a house named Fern Villa, at 26 Eastnor Street, near to Old Trafford Police Station and not far from the tramway into central Manchester. Their first son, Louis, was born at home on 24 April 1883 and later that year, they moved along the street to number 22. Known as 'the playground of Manchester', Old Trafford was enjoying the final years of its heyday and the wealthy lived in elegant villas, still overlooking green pastures and farmland. Local landowners like the de Trafford family had encouraged the development of cultural and leisure facilities, such as the Old Trafford Botanical Gardens, which opened to the public in 1831 and hosted the Art Treasures Exhibition in 1857. Its biggest event would be the Royal Jubilee Exhibition, attended by Queen Victoria in May 1887. Other attractions included the Pomona Gardens, with its impressive glasshouse, and the Manchester Cricket Club (now the Lancashire Cricket Club).

This salubrious district began to attract the professional middle classes who aspired to a superior quality of life, away from the grime and smoke of the city, especially as transport links improved access to the centre. As a well-paid police inspector, Detective Caminada was one of these new urban residents. He also became a landlord, purchasing a number of houses in neighbouring Lucy Street, which he let. However, despite Mr and Mrs Caminada's cosy new life in the suburbs, crime was never far away and it would not be long before a shady character came knocking at their door.

On Tuesday 18 March 1884, the Caminada family were enjoying a rare morning together at their home. A delicate child, baby Louis was sleeping after his lunch when the doorbell rang. Jerome opened the door to find a 'stylishly dressed man, fluent in speech' on his doorstep, whom he recognised as accomplished swindler, 'Handsome Charlie'. Clearly failing to recall Caminada, Handsome Charlie brandished a letter about a loan, which he claimed had allegedly come from the astonished detective. After Caminada had invited him into the house to discuss the matter, Handsome Charlie explained that he wished to borrow £50, for which he would pay £10 interest for one month. He was at pains to add that the loan was for his friend, on whose behalf he was making enquiries. After reassuring Caminada that his friend had securities in the London and North Western Railway and the Bridgewater Canal, Caminada arranged for the friend to call the following afternoon.

At 2pm the next day, Caminada found an elderly, well-dressed gentleman squinting at the house number in the strong sunlight. Surprised that Handsome Charlie's accomplice had actually turned up, Caminada invited him inside. The gentleman was John Mosley, 60, a tobacconist from Ardwick, one mile east of the city centre. Mosley said that he had £150 to draw at the end of the month, and would leave some valuables as security for the loan, including a gold watch and chain (a gift from his daughter), three rings and several pawn tickets. After Mosley emptied his pockets, Caminada revealed his true identity: 'Now, my friend, you can leave the jewellery here and go and bring your friend "George the Greek". If you do not I will have you locked up for attempting to defraud me out of fifty pounds by means of worthless jewellery'. George the Greek was another daring swindler and a known associate of Mosley and Handsome Charlie.

The elderly gentleman's response was to jump up, stamp his feet and slap the table in indignation. Despite the fact that this was taking place in his home, with his wife and child nearby, Caminada remained calm. He called to Amelia, who was in the next room, to bring him the cash box, which quietened Mosley down. Caminada took out pen and paper to write a promissory note for £60, payable the following day. Furious that the detective had not handed over any cash, Mosley flew once again into a violent rage. Caminada, after first putting on his hat, seized the swindler by the collar and dragged him to Old Trafford Police Station.

Leaving Mosley in custody he then went to his address in Ardwick, only to discover that Mosley and Handsome Charlie were neighbours and used each other's addresses to defraud potential victims and evade arrest. This time their game was up: Mosley was found guilty and sentenced to six months' imprisonment with hard labour. A warrant was issued for the arrest of Handsome Charlie, but he managed to avoid the law for the time being. Later it was revealed that a neighbour had written the letter with the detective's address, to lure the con man straight into a trap.

While criminals rarely came knocking on his door, Detective Caminada's keen instinct for scams often saved him from being robbed. He once prevented a large-scale fraud that touched even the town hall and the local police constabulary.

Caminada and his wife regularly had coal delivered to their house and, keeping a strict eye on domestic expenditure, the detective was in the habit of checking the amount delivered. Examining his cellar one day he became suspicious; the two tons of coal usually delivered should fill his cellar, but this time, an additional two hundredweight had apparently been required to replenish the same space. Unwilling to let it pass without investigation, Caminada went directly to the wharf to order the next load from the proprietor, who was a neighbour and close friend. After questioning the weight of the previous supply, he arranged a delivery for a new consignment of their 'best' coal. The foreman made out the order in the presence of the detective and this time only one ton and 18 hundredweights filled the cellar.

His suspicions confirmed, Caminada now had to find proof of the coal agent's double dealing: 'I determined to be even with the coal merchant, even if I waited 20 years for an opportunity'. He did not have to wait long. Having emptied his cellar of every last lump of coal, he arranged the next delivery for 7am the following Thursday. When the appointed time arrived he watched out for the carter in the garden, but he did not turn up and Caminada had to leave for work. When he returned home later, the coal had already been delivered.

Despite this setback, the detective persisted and a week later he took one of the carters to a local alehouse for a drink. During their conversation he discovered that a disagreement had taken place between the proprietor and the carters over stoppage of pay during Whit Week and they had decided to take industrial action. This was Caminada's opportunity to strike at the heart of this dubious business. After interviewing several more disgruntled carters, he found that there were two systems of issuing tickets, one set giving the correct weight and another, with two or three hundredweights added, the latter being in operation when the customer had no means of checking. In addition, the coal merchant often sold interier quality 'seconds' coal at the same price as 'best'.

After amassing enough evidence, Caminada arrested the proprietor, his manager, the foreman and the clerk. The manager, who was also the son-in-law of the owner, declared that the responsibility was entirely his and, after a protracted trial, they were all convicted of conspiracy to defraud, except the proprietor, who was acquitted but had to pay the legal expenses. In his summing up, the judge complimented Caminada on his 'detective qualities'. The coal merchant had gained contracts to supply fuel, not only to the Caminada household, but also to the Corporation of Manchester at the Town Hall, to the Police Court and to police stations throughout the city. Caminada's suspicions were justified:

> *Thus the Corporation, amongst others, received the benefit of the exposure and prosecution, whilst I had the satisfaction of knowing that I had broken down a conspiracy which had not spared even my own fireside.*

Detective Caminada and his wife were now settled in their comfortable house in Old Trafford and life had improved for the rest of his family too, although not quite to the same extent. By the mid-1870s, Caminada's mother, Mary, had left the rookeries of central Manchester and moved to Barton upon Irwell, about five miles from Jerome. Barton was a suburb of Salford and, although the area was predominantly populated by textile workers, Mary no longer had to share her home with several other families. In 1881, aged 66, she was living with her daughter Teresa, 28, who still worked as a silk winder in a local factory. Five years earlier, Teresa had given birth to an illegitimate daughter, Annie, who also lived with them. There was no father named on her birth certificate.

Although life was better, Mary still had major challenges to face. The census revealed that she had lost her sight and her blindness was likely to have been a tertiary stage symptom of syphilis, which seems to have blighted her adult life and the lives of her children.

Mary's other surviving child, John Baptiste, had spent most of his adult life away from home, but things had not been any easier for him. In the early 1860s, he had moved to Newcastle-upon-Lyme, where he worked as a letter carrier for the British Postal Service. In 1868 he married Kezia Skey, a farmer's daughter originally from Gloucestershire, and later that year she gave birth to twins, Louis and Teresa. Aged just five weeks, Teresa had died of marasmus, a wasting disease, usually due to severe malnutrition and often an indication of inherited syphilis. Teresa's twin brother survived and the couple had another child, Florence Mary, who would later become inextricably linked with one of her Uncle Jerome's most famous cases.

By the early 1880s, John Baptiste and his family had returned to Manchester and settled in Cheetham, another densely populated area of mill workers near the centre of the city and the location of the forbidding Strangeways Prison. John worked as a druggist, making and supplying pills and other chemicals from his home.

In Victorian England, many impoverished families like the Caminadas left British shores for a new life abroad. From the end of the Napoleonic Wars in

1815 to the beginning of the Great Depression in 1929, 11.4 million people made the momentous decision to emigrate to countries such as America, Canada and Australia, which were then British colonies. Many took advantage of government-assisted passage schemes, which encouraged workers from impoverished rural communities and insalubrious urban conditions to take their chances elsewhere, in the hope of a better quality of life.

During the summer of 1884, Detective Caminada exposed a treacherous scam which exploited the aspirations of the poor in Manchester. Advertisements appeared on placards throughout the city publicising The British Employment, Emigration and Aid Society, which claimed to provide opportunities for work overseas by setting people up in the colonies as farmers. The proprietor, Walter Hamilton, ran his operation from impressively furnished offices in the city centre, where he held lectures on the benefits of emigration, collected subscriptions and received endorsements from prominent citizens, including the Bishop of Manchester. Attractive prospectuses and penny pamphlets filled with stories of enterprise and success, drew flocks of people, many of whom then bought tickets for a passage abroad. Before long, however, the naïve victims discovered that this promise was a sham.

Complaints started to come into the detective office and armed with several witness statements, Caminada arrested Hamilton while he was holding forth in the middle of one of his lectures in Burnley Marketplace. He later found Hamilton's phony pamphlets and other incriminating evidence at his premises. The sophisticated swindler was convicted and sentenced to five years' penal servitude. Caminada commented wryly that, had the transportation of criminals to the colonies still been in vogue at that time, Hamilton would have been able to 'realise his dream of emigration free of cost to himself'. Following his conviction, Caminada discovered, among Hamilton's papers, a letter from three sisters who had travelled from Ireland to participate in the fake emigration scheme. They were just 10, 16 and 19 years old and had sold everything they owned in their bid for a new life overseas. Moved by their plight, Caminada started a subscription for them, raising £12 (around £1,000 today). He also obtained clothing from some local ladies and secured the young women a passage to Canada.

As the emigration scam was reaching its conclusion, Caminada was promoted to Detective Chief Inspector in June 1884. But at home, he and his wife were about to experience dark times reminiscent of his own early years. Just three weeks after his promotion, baby Louis died. Aged 14 months, his death was attributed to congenital heart disease, an inherited condition which had killed Jerome's father almost 40 years before.

After Louis's death, Amelia quickly fell pregnant again and their daughter was born the following spring on 9 April 1885. Another sickly child, she died at just six weeks old of 'general debility': a catch-all phrase that indicated the absence of a clear diagnosis. Just over a year later, their third child, Charles, was born in September 1886, yet in a cruel twist of fate, on Christmas Day, the anniversary of the deaths of two of Caminada's siblings, Charles died, aged four months. He too had suffered from a congenital heart condition. Losing three children in as many years must have been devastating for Jerome and Amelia. They buried their babies in the family grave in Southern Cemetery, a large municipal graveyard in southern Manchester. The poignant inscription reads: 'Suffer the little children to come unto me and forbid them not, for of such is the Kingdom of Heaven' (Mark 10:14).

Despite these terrible losses during their early family life, the Caminadas went on to have two more children and were eventually able to enjoy their secure and prosperous home. But for many in Manchester, home was not a place of refuge. Every week, after toiling long hours in the mills and factories, people flocked to the beerhouses and gin palaces to drink away their sorrows, causing endless trouble for Detective Caminada and his colleagues, as they sought to keep the peace on the turbulent streets of the city.

Chapter Seven

Gin Palaces, Gambling Dens and a Cross-Dressing Ball (1885)

The gin-shops are in full feather – their swinging doors never hang a moment still. Itinerant bands blow and bang their loudest; organ boys grind monotonously; ballad singers or flying stationers make roaring proclamations of their wares. The street is one swarming, buzzing mass of people.
(Angus Bethune Reach, *Morning Chronicle*, 1849)

During the nineteenth century, Manchester city centre was a magnet for revellers, and Saturday night was the high point of the week. Ready to spend their weekly wages, workers flocked into the beerhouses, music saloons, theatres and taverns for a night out to forget their daily grind. Everyone was out to have a good time and nocturnal entertainment knew no bounds.

Detective Caminada was no stranger to the hectic nightlife in his home city, especially as he had spent his early years in Peter Street, the heart of Manchester's theatreland. Near to his birthplace was St Peter's Square with a concert hall and casino. On his former street there was the Folly Theatre (later re-named the Tivoli), an early music hall, converted from a Methodist chapel in 1865, and the Theatre Royal, one of the first theatres in the city, which opened in 1815. Next door is the Free Trade Hall, the former home of the Hallé Orchestra, founded in 1857, and a place where Caminada solved a rather unusual case.

A complaint was made about sheets of music being stolen from the Free Trade Hall. Every night during the concerts, music would disappear with the thief leaving no clues behind as to their identity. Caminada arranged to have a large, fake piano box made with discreet holes cut in it, so he could hide inside it and observe what was going on. On the evening of the next concert, he was in position when the musicians went out onto the stage, leaving the conductor and the librarian, who was in charge of the music, in the anteroom. Both men were above the slightest suspicion. At 7.30pm, the conductor joined his orchestra and the concert began. Under the vigilant eye of Caminada nothing untoward took place until the second half of the performance, when the librarian started rifling through the music. His eyes widened as he spotted a piece that grabbed his attention. Scanning the room to make sure that he was alone, the librarian slipped two sheets from the pile into his pocket.

After the concert, the anteroom filled with musicians. They leant their instruments against the piano box, while the librarian congratulated them. He bid them goodnight as they gradually left. Only Caminada remained and, when the gasman appeared to extinguish the lights, the detective realised that he was in a fix and needed help to get out of the box. Unable to think of a better plan, he cried out, 'Shift these fiddles!' his voice echoing in the confined space. Trembling and with his hair standing on end, the gasman stared at the violins in fright, before hurriedly lifting his stick to finish his nightly duties. Caminada called out again: 'Shift these fiddles from the piano case, man, and let me out. I'm no ghost, but flesh and blood like yourself'.

With his mouth gaping open and perspiration on his brow, the gasman opened the box and watched in terror as the detective clambered out. The case solved, Caminada tried to explain the situation to the poor man, but he refused to listen and apparently never spoke of his 'ghostly' experience again. The fate of the light-fingered librarian is unknown.

Amongst the glitzy theatres and lively music halls of Manchester were many seedier venues of entertainment – gin shops, brothels, gambling dens and beerhouses – all of which enjoyed a flourishing trade. The Beerhouse Act of 1830 allowed anyone to brew and sell beer on purchase of a licence for two guineas, which led to the opening of numerous beerhouses, especially in the industrial north of England. Beersellers brewed barrels of beer, which they sold in the front room of their houses for a few pennies.

In the rookeries of Manchester there were several drinking dens on every street, many operating from the parlours of terraced houses. Beer was served from a rough counter and the drinkers sat at small tables on wooden benches. The rooms were dark and stuffy, the air acrid with tobacco smoke. Drinking would be accompanied by lively tunes on accordions, barrel organs and pianos, continuing into the early hours of the morning. The grander establishments held more organised entertainment, including musical and theatrical acts on a stage. Known as the 'free and easy', individuals would take turns to perform in an early form of variety show. The beerhouses, on the other hand, also offered less innocent activities, such as illegal prize fighting, dog fighting, gambling and prostitution.

In 1832 Dr James Kay reported in *The moral and physical condition of the working classes employed in the cotton manufacture in Manchester*, that there were 430 licensed tavern and innkeepers in the city and 322 gin shops, mostly in the poorest districts. Friedrich Engels recounted the aftermath of a typical night out at these establishments in *The Condition of the Working Class in England in 1844*:

> *On Saturday evenings, especially when wages are paid and work stops somewhat earlier than usual, when the whole working-class pours from its own poor quarters into the main thoroughfares, intemperance may be seen in all its brutality. I have rarely come out of Manchester on such an evening without meeting numbers of people staggering and seeing others lying in the gutter.*

By 1853 the number of beerhouses in Manchester had risen to over 1,500 and it continued to increase throughout the century. Excessive drinking often led to crime and the police returns of 1874 reveal that drunkenness accounted for nearly a half of all offences committed. Other crimes such as breach of the peace, assault, wilful damage, and not least, prostitution, were also fuelled by alcohol consumption. The police had a real battle on their hands and Detective Caminada did not shrink from playing his part.

At 3am one Monday, Caminada was on duty. He was standing on the corner of Great Bridgewater Street, not far from the canal, when he saw two men coming towards him from an oyster shop across the street. The proprietor of the shop was known as 'Flecky Sam' (meaning 'dirty') because he always wore the same clothes. He and his pet monkey, an accomplished pickpocket, did a roaring trade after the pubs closed in the early hours.

The two intoxicated men, 'Leeds Jemmy' and 'The Badger', wished the detective a slurred 'Good morning', as they passed by. Caminada began to follow them and, thinking that he was a teetotaller or city missionary, the men hurled abuse at him. Caminada arrested them, but all he found in their pockets was an Irish harp halfpenny and a copper coin which had been defaced with a chisel. They were released with a caution.

Later that morning, Caminada received information about a burglary in a grocer's shop. When he investigated, he discovered that the shop had been securely fastened and the cellar door tied with a rope. The burglars had entered the cellar via the street grid and then prised open the door, enough to throw a lighted piece of paper through the gap to burn through the rope. The grocer could not identify the robbers, but he recognised the coins that Caminada had confiscated earlier from the two drunken men. Leeds Jemmy and the Badger were both sentenced to 18 months' imprisonment and, from the dock, Jemmy vowed that he would 'do' for the detective on his release.

He was as good as his word and one Sunday morning, when Caminada was walking down Charter Street in the heart of the slums, Leeds Jemmy rushed out of the house of 'Cabbage Ann', a disreputable thief and receiver of stolen goods, and punched the detective in the head. A crowd gathered round, cheering as the two men fought in the street. In the middle of the battle, Joseph, the son of another fence, 'One-Armed Kitty', rushed out with a bottle and threw it at Caminada, who fortunately ducked at the right moment. The missile, however, struck the helmet of another police officer and he fell to the ground, with blood pouring from his head. Fearing that he had killed the officer, Joseph fled up a nearby alley, closely pursued by Caminada. The throng followed and surrounded the detective, punching him from all sides. Caminada somehow managed to escape, but by that time Leeds Jemmy had disappeared.

A fortnight later, Leeds Jemmy and The Badger were arrested, after breaking into a house next door to Henshaw's Blind Asylum. They had led the police a merry dance, including diving into the Bridgewater Canal. This time, they both received seven years' penal servitude.

Like most working-class men at the time, Detective Caminada enjoyed a drink and often invited an informant or a prospective witness to an alehouse, to exchange information over a glass of beer. Although he was resolute in his condemnation of beerhouses, he had sympathy for those who resorted to alcohol to escape their lot in life:

> *I yield to none in my advocacy of temperance, but I say there is a poverty in our midst which is not caused by drink. I do not say that there is not a great deal of poverty caused by drink, or greatly increased by drink, but where we have people living like this we must not be surprised if they are attracted to the glittering gin-palaces for their warmth and company. I often wonder that things are not ten times worse than they are.*

Sadly, Caminada would experience the effect of alcohol closer to home, when his older brother, John Baptiste, died in 1902, of 'disease caused by excessive drinking'.

By the end of the nineteenth century, the police had begun in earnest to tackle the problems of drink-related crime on the streets of Manchester. Detective Caminada was singlehandedly responsible for closing more than 400 disreputable beerhouses. However, many drinking establishments masqueraded as respectable social clubs but were, in reality, illegal gambling dens. To combat this Caminada masterminded a raid on the city's clubs, which was unprecedented in scale and effectiveness, and significantly contributed to reducing alcohol-fuelled offences.

Hailed in the local newspapers as 'The Great Raid', this 'masterly attack' on illegal gambling clubs was a first in the history of the city. According to the *Manchester Courier*, it was also long overdue: 'These houses have been a crying nuisance and a shameful disgrace to the city for some years'. Detective Inspector Caminada had been preparing for the raid for months, by placing informants throughout the network of 22 betting clubs. On 21 May 1885, the second day of the Newmarket Spring race meeting, when many of the gambling clubs would be in full swing, Caminada gathered 400 officers together at 1pm, ready for the raid. The operation relied on surprise and precise timing, as the clubs were connected by telephone and would be able to alert each other of a raid within minutes. Leading the largest contingent of 170 officers, Caminada had organised a special task force for each club headed by a detective, so that the attack would be simultaneous.

The betting clubs were usually run by one individual, often a well-to-do businessman. Each syndicate had 300 to 400 members, paying an annual subscription of between one and three shillings, many including women and children as subscribers. On the premises, there would be typically a bar selling beer and spirits, billiard tables, comfortable chairs and telegraphic equipment. As well as betting on horses, there were other gambling games, such as cards. These clubs were unregulated, unregistered and entirely illegal.

On the afternoon of 21 May, the atmosphere was tense as Caminada and his squad arrived at the first two clubs: the Rous and the Falmouth. Both clubs occupied the same premises, on the ground and first floors of a building next to the Falstaff Hotel, near the old marketplace. Caminada broke down the door and uniformed officers entered first, causing complete chaos as bookmakers and managers tried to hide their books and betting sheets. Plain-clothes detectives climbed the winding staircase, meeting the owners as they tried to leave and there was considerable damage to 'hats and heads' in the scramble for freedom. Several individuals tried to escape by jumping out of windows. As one unfortunate man leaped onto a skylight the roof fell in, landing him straight back in the clubroom. He then jumped through a window and sustained a serious cut to his leg.

Nearly all the windows were smashed, as 200 gamblers sought to evade the police. In a loud voice over the mayhem, Caminada read out the warrant reassuring the punters that they would not be arrested and were free to leave. Order was restored and the officials of the clubs were apprehended, while the clients made their exit. Around 20 men were taken into custody and escorted to the town hall.

Outside, the whole city had been roused and a large crowd had gathered. Excitement mounted as the police departed with their prisoners. The horde surged through the streets, shouting and jeering after Caminada and his colleagues, as they made their way to their next target. The officers swept through several more clubs during the course of the afternoon, arresting the operators. One of the largest betting houses was The Russel Club, which had about 700 members. As he entered, Caminada identified the owner and gave the order: 'Handcuff the man in the Cardigan jacket'. The next on the list was the Devonshire. Located over a stable and accessed via a wooden stepladder from a coach house, it was a favourite haunt of the wives of workingmen and they made up a substantial number of its 370 members.

One of the worst gambling dens was the Central Club in Back Lad Lane, Deansgate. Housed in a large room that opened out onto the roof, it had a dirty floor covered in sawdust and a rickety billiard table. The dank air was blue with cigarette smoke. About 70 rough characters were there, almost all shabbily dressed. As one of the bookmakers, known as 'Young Cheeky', was taken into custody, he insisted on helping himself to a thick cigar and a drink, tucking a meat pie under his arm for later.

Towards the end of the day the police officers arrived at the Lancashire Club on the edge of the city. By this time the crowd was immense and the detectives led the prisoners from the club, accompanied by street musicians playing 'Auld Lang Syne', and 'We'll Run Them In', from the 'Gendarmes Duet' by Offenbach. Local newspapers like the *Manchester Courier* were full of praise for the city's police: 'If this raid is the means of stopping even this most degrading system, it will have secured an end worthy of double such an effort'.

The ensuing police proceedings were widely reported and the *Sporting Chronicle* printed a rare description of Detective Caminada:

The celebrated Manchester detective, whose name and fame are known from one end of England to the other, is nothing very dreadful to look at; indeed, some people might describe him – and with truth – as a pleasant little man. He might be a trifle over 5ft 7in in height, but not much more, while his weight, at a rough guess, would be 12st or 13st. Caminada wears a moustache, and a thin fringing beard and whiskers give the impression that a razor has seldom, if ever, visited his broad, good-humoured face, while he parts his hair down the centre, and does not appear to have a particle of ill-nature about him.

Under examination Caminada's answers come out short, sharp and decisive, with a certain "snap" about his words as if he was putting handcuffs on everything he says, to make his replies thoroughly secure. He has in every instance a clear tale to tell, with powers of terse description, and a condensed summing up of what he sees and does which are simply perfect.

On 30 July, the watch committee awarded Caminada a £50 bonus 'in consideration of his valuable services' and his salary was increased from £150 to £200 per annum. He had carried out one of the most successful police raids in the history of the city, but there was one other notable raid still to come, the like of which he and his fellow officers had never experienced before.

The police received a tip-off that an event 'of an immoral character' was about to take place in the Temperance Hall in Hulme. An unknown party, supposedly acting under the auspices of the Association of Pawnbrokers' Assistants had hired the building, which seated 120 people, for a ball. When the chief constable obtained confidential information as to the nature of the evening's entertainment, he instructed Detective Caminada to keep a sharp watch on the proceedings.

Late on a Friday evening, Caminada positioned plain-clothes and uniformed officers in the vicinity of the hall. At 9pm cabs began to arrive, the occupants of which were all male. Many of them were carrying portmanteaus or large tin boxes which they dragged into the building. Some were dressed in female attire, including low-cut ball gowns, whilst others were wearing theatrical costumes of a historical nature: this was no ordinary ball. Caminada counted 47 men attending the dance, 22 of whom were dressed as women. Dancing began at 10pm, accompanied by an orchestra conducted by a blind harmonium player. The windows of the hall had been screened with calico and paper to prevent onlookers, except for one that was left partially uncovered for ventilation. Caminada climbed the roof of an adjoining building where, from behind a chimneystack, he observed the dancers' activities through the open window. The *Nottingham Evening Post* reported that the company was engaged in 'grotesque dances, such as are familiar at low-class music halls'.

Satisfied that crimes were being committed, Caminada gave the signal for a raid at just before 1am. A dozen officers surrounded the building and when they were in place Caminada knocked several times at the door, until someone called out, 'Who's there?' The detective replied in a feminine voice with the password 'Sister' and a man dressed as a Sister of Mercy opened the door. The police rushed in, only to be attacked by several of the dancers and even Caminada was hurled backwards. Quickly regaining his composure, he seized the two men nearest to him and set about making arrests. Some of the men had managed to remove their dresses in the fracas. Others tried to escape through the windows, but were foiled by police on the ground. Calling on the services of some workingmen nearby, Caminada rounded up the prisoners, who were handcuffed and taken in small groups to the town hall, along with several cab-loads of clothing as evidence.

Later that day in court, Detective Caminada confirmed the identity of the prisoners, whom he considered were mainly 'of vicious character'. Although their friends had supplied them with ordinary clothes, some of the defendants still had dyed hair. The prosecuting barrister, Mr Cobbett, called the event 'one of the foulest and most disgraceful orgies that ever reproached a town'. The presiding magistrate commented that he was relieved to discover that the majority of the men were from Sheffield, rather than Manchester. The participants of the cross-dressing ball were charged with misdemeanour and remanded in custody.

As male homosexual acts were then still illegal – carrying the death penalty until 1861 – illicit meetings had to be held underground. 'Molly houses' had been in existence since the eighteenth century. These were held in private rooms, coffee houses or taverns, where cross-dressing men could socialise in safety. Homosexual men and transvestites also met in theatrical public houses and private gentlemen's clubs, particularly in places like the West End of London. Such a large-scale occasion as the cross-dressing ball in Manchester was quite rare, as the risk of exposure was high even though punishment for the offence, by this time, had been downgraded to imprisonment.

This unusual experience must have afforded Detective Caminada a lighter moment in his otherwise intense and often dangerous police work.

Following the dazzling success of the betting club raids in 1885, he would come up against the challenging case of the Birmingham Forger. This long-running saga would lead to a personal vendetta by a witness and a series of complex trials, where the detective would eventually find himself in the dock.

Chapter Eight

The Birmingham Forger
(1886–1887)

An extremely smart capture was made yesterday in this city by Chief Detective Inspector Caminada, of the Manchester force. About noon, as the officer was standing near the Bank of England, King-street, his attention was attracted to a man who was loitering about the bank. The man appeared to Caminada to resemble an individual whose portrait appeared in last week's Police Gazette, and who was wanted by the Birmingham police on serious charges of forgery and theft.

(*Manchester Evening News*, 7 December 1886)

When Chief Inspector Caminada arrested the Birmingham Forger on 6 December 1886 outside the Queen's Theatre in Manchester, he was unaware that this complicated case would have some surprising twists and turns, including an attention-seeking witness and a spurned lover. Worse still, a legal battle connected with the case would cast a shadow over the detective's career, long after the conviction of Arthur Foster.

At the end of November 1886 Caminada was enjoying a holiday with his wife and baby son Charles, in the Derbyshire spa town of Buxton. When his two-month-old son's precarious health began to deteriorate, the family returned home. En route Caminada dropped in at the town hall to see if anything had been 'stirring' in his absence. While he was there, Superintendent Hicks told him about George Tracey, a man from the colonies, who had reported the theft of an expensive bracelet and was offering a reward of £20 for its recovery. Shortly after, Tracey had called in again to inform the police that the bracelet had been found entangled in the dress of the lady who owned it.

The superintendent felt there was something shifty about the man and reported to Caminada that he was clean-shaven, wore a wig and resembled the actor Henry Irving. His circumstances were also dubious: Tracey had said that he was from San Francisco, but was now residing in the rough neighbourhood of Greenheys on the edge of Manchester. Caminada confirmed the superintendent's suspicions:

It appeared to me that Carter Street was not a neighbourhood where bracelets of the value of £120 were ordinarily found, and I remarked to the Superintendent, "If he lives in Carter Street, Greenheys, and says that he has come from San Francisco, there is something 'dickey' about him and inquiries should be made at once.

His curiosity aroused, Caminada set off immediately to make enquiries. He soon discovered that Tracey was a clerk, involved in the preparations for a pantomime and also associated with a local house of theatrical ladies. After sounding out his usual informants, Caminada returned to the town hall, where he bumped into a shopkeeper who was leaving. Henry Pingstone had just reported a mysterious customer in his hosiery store. The client looked like a priest or an actor, and had bought a new suit for £15 in a suspiciously ostentatious manner. When Pingstone gave the man's name as George Tracey, Caminada knew he had a lead. Yet, before long he would bitterly regret that Pingstone had ever become involved in the case.

Henry Pingstone was a linen draper and hosier with a shop on Market Street, in Manchester's commercial district. He was also a member of the city council. Despite his initial enthusiasm to give information about Tracey, he soon tried to dissociate himself from the formal investigation, by insisting that his name was kept confidential. Caminada reassured Pingstone that he was prepared to act on information gleaned, without revealing the identity of his sources: 'If I had to wait for definite information in every case, one half of the criminals would escape me'. After their first meeting, Caminada accompanied Pingstone back to his shop and then took up position in a doorway opposite. Fifteen minutes later, Tracey appeared and the detective followed him through the streets to the Bank of England, where he changed a large amount of gold into cash.

After shadowing Tracey all afternoon, Caminada returned to the detective office, where he assembled his colleagues and, producing an image of a woodcut from the previous week's edition of the *Police Gazette,* he suggested that Tracey was in fact Arthur Foster, wanted for forgery in Birmingham. The other officers were not convinced but, sticking to his instincts, Caminada went to Greenheys with the picture in his pocket and trailed Foster and his glamorous lady companion into the Queen's Theatre for the evening's performance of *The World.* While watching the play, the detective knew that he had his man:

Tracey, who followed the plot of the piece and the fate of the diamonds with the closest interest, was apparently overjoyed at the triumph of the robber

who effected his purpose by administering chloroform. As he leaned back in
the box laughing, I looked again at the portrait and decided to arrest him.

As reported in the *Manchester Evening News*, Foster's choice of play 'adds a somewhat dramatic feature to the arrest'.

Back at the town hall, the prisoner denied that he was Foster, but when Caminada threatened to send a telegraph to the Birmingham Police Force he agreed to co-operate, on the condition that his lady-friend was released. Before leaving, the woman handed over the diamond bracelet, apparently a gift from Foster, along with other jewels: two gold rings; another diamond-encrusted bracelet; earrings and brooches set with pearls; a gold necklet and locket; a gold watch; and an ivory fan.

Foster admitted the charges and a search of his person yielded £320 in notes, £12 in gold, £14 in silver, two diamond rings, a gold watch with an albert chain and a pearl and diamond stud set in gold. Foster had been on a spending spree. Stripped of his jewels, the prisoner was charged, but not content with the heist so far, Caminada returned to Foster's lodgings to search for more stolen goods.

In Greenheys, after persuading the landlady to open Foster's bedroom door, the detective discovered nearly £4,000 in new gold coins in a leather portmanteau and £26 stashed in a small leather bag (around £350,000 today).

After the widely-reported arrest, some intriguing new details came to light in the newspapers. According to the *Birmingham Daily Post*, a previous 'flame' had betrayed Foster to the police. The mystery woman had arranged to meet him the evening before his night out at the theatre and, when he failed to turn up, she was furious. Learning that he had 'taken up' with the Vanishing Lady, she had sent a photograph of him to the detective office in revenge and intimated that he was up to no good. The Vanishing Lady, Foster's companion at the time of his arrest, was an actress appearing at the Free Trade Hall in the show of celebrated mesmerist, T. A. Kennedy, who used hypnotism to 'nightly provoke continuous merriment'. In the newspapers, she was described as a woman of 'more or less doubtful character'.

Clearly popular with women, 33-year-old Arthur Foster had already enjoyed a notable career as a thief and a forger, but he had also spent more than a third of his life in prison. Using several aliases, including George Tracey, he had committed a number of offences of forgery and embezzlement, and already completed almost 12 years of penal servitude. Undeterred by prison, as soon as he was freed on ticket-of-leave (probation) in February 1885, he had returned to his former tricks. However, at first Foster was employed as a newspaper reporter in Shrewsbury. This did not last long and, by the summer, he had forged references to obtain a position as a clerk with solicitor, Isaac Bradley, in preparation for carrying out his most daring theft yet.

For a while Foster kept his head down and worked hard. Bradley would later refer to him in court as 'industrious and sober'. However, towards the end of October, assuming the alias of 'Walter Nicholls', Foster made arrangements with Bradley's London agent, John Thomas White, to receive a claim amounting to £5,200 from Chancery on behalf of a client. Formal letters were exchanged, signatures were checked and the agent handed over the cash to 'Nicholls', who immediately absconded. White offered a reward of £200 for recovery of the money.

This sophisticated fraud was carried out with great skill and Foster might have got away with it, had it not been for the instinct and determination of Jerome Caminada. Arthur Foster was convicted of forgery at the Old Bailey. At the sentencing he appealed for mercy on the grounds that 'he yielded to temptation' but, despite his pleas, he received 15 years' imprisonment. The case of the Birmingham Forger was closed and for Detective Caminada a new battle was about to begin.

Despite the shopkeeper Henry Pingstone's initial reluctance to become involved, when he realised that Tracey was the Birmingham Forger, he became keen to help the police with their enquiries, even insisting on a place in the city police court, where he could watch the proceedings without being seen. The police congratulated Pingstone on his valuable contribution to the case and Caminada naïvely suggested that he receive a handsome gratuity for his assistance. But Pingstone wanted more. Launching a campaign to secure the reward of £200 previously offered by the deceived London agent, John White, he wrote letters to the newspapers demanding credit for the arrest. The watch committee and the city council also put in petitions for payment of the reward. Messrs White and Sons paid the money into the court but then a complex legal battle commenced, with Councillor Pingstone going head-to-head with Chief Inspector Caminada.

Pingstone's line of reasoning was that his information had led directly to Foster's arrest, while Caminada contested that the investigation had already been under way before Pingstone became involved. During the first trial, on 5 May 1887, the judge complimented the detective as 'a tolerably determined officer'. In his summing up he said:

every credit is due to Caminada for the intelligence and firmness and decision with which he acted; because…he, with great sagacity, determined that he was the right man and so secured a very serious offender.

Pingstone, on the other hand, was seen as excitable and over-zealous in his desire to take part in the police operations. The judge intimated that he might be an attention-seeker: 'It may be a satisfaction to the pride of some people to have their names mixed up with the detection and arrest of criminals'. Despite his comments, the jury found for Pingstone, but the detective was not finished with the interfering shopkeeper.

Following an appeal, Caminada was granted a second trial on the grounds that the jury 'had taken a wrong view of the facts'. The hearing, before a special jury, took place at the Manchester Assizes over a year after the original case of the Birmingham Forger. This time Pingstone presented an almost comic figure in court and the judge ordered him to stand up, instead of lolling in the witness box. Once again the judge considered Pingstone's involvement in the case to be superficial and self-aggrandising: 'he was delighted that he had a finger in the pie, that he helped to catch this great thief'. In concluding, Mr Justice Grantham gave his perceptive opinion of the case: 'I cannot help feeling that had this been a contest between other persons than a town councillor and a member of the police force, you would not have been troubled with this case at all'.

The result of the second trial was that the reward should be shared between both parties, as well as the costs of the trials. Detective Caminada had to find £185, a not inconsiderable sum, when his annual salary was £200.

It was customary for Victorian police officers to receive rewards following the positive resolution of important cases. After the 1835 Municipal Corporations Act, watch committees were established to manage local police forces. The Manchester Borough Watch Committee was founded in 1839. Composed of elected members of the local council, the committee was responsible for promotions and rewards, as well as demotions and fines of individual police officers. In addition, private businesses and individuals could reward the police for successfully resolving specific crimes. Where appropriate, it was the role of the chief constable to divide up rewards and distribute them accordingly. Sometimes he chose to place them into the police superannuation scheme.

During his 30-year career Detective Caminada received many rewards from the Manchester Borough Watch Committee and private businesses for his sterling detective work, usually between £20 and £100. It was estimated in the *Police Review* that he received a total of just £400 from the watch committee, even though he had secured payment, on their behalf, of more than £9,300 in fines, following arrests.

Following the Pingstone case, Caminada's supporters rallied round and held a meeting at the Queen's Hotel to start a fund. Enough money was raised to pay the detective's legal costs with an extra 300 guineas which they presented to him for the benefit of his family. Whilst this case had been unfolding, Jerome and his wife had experienced the sad death of their baby son Charles. A year later, just before the second trial against Henry Pingstone, Amelia had given birth to a fourth child. Another son, he was named Charles Bernard and would survive to adulthood.

After two complicated trials, this difficult situation ended well for Detective Caminada, but Henry Pingstone would have the final word. The egotistical witness had his own group of supporters, who also raised money to pay his share of the costs. At his presentation at the Victoria Hotel, they gloated over Pingstone's triumph in the courts, praising him as 'a man who has pluckily fought a public battle, and secured from a jury a verdict in his favour, which verdict, if left unchallenged, would have given others encouragement to give our detectives wrinkles that might oftener lead to the arrest of those who live upon their wits and our money'. As the chairman of the fundraising committee handed over the cheque to the proud shopkeeper, he commented that 'Mr Pingstone had passed through a fiery furnace which had tested his metal. They all appreciated the vigour and pertinacity with which he held to what he believed to be a public right'.

Detective Caminada had been harassed by Henry Pingstone for almost two years, but Pingstone was nothing compared to the man he was about to tackle next. Bob Horridge was a ruthless career criminal, whom Caminada had first arrested while he was a police constable. Released in 1887, Horridge was determined to exact revenge on the detective and to end their rivalry once and for all.

Chapter Nine

'The Professor Moriarty of the Slums'
(1887)

*As to the reformation of the criminal, that is a myth; the prison is the best
school of crime which we possess.*
(Jerome Caminada, *Twenty-Five Years of Detective Life*, 1901)

Bob Horridge, one of the most desperate criminals that Caminada ever
encountered, was an unscrupulous felon hardened by time spent
behind bars, and the detective's own real-life 'Professor Moriarty'.
An expert thief, Horridge terrorised the streets of Manchester for more
than two decades. After his first long prison sentence, his career of crime
began in earnest and it would eventually lead to a deadly showdown with his
nemesis, Detective Caminada.

Robert Charles Horridge was born on 20 July 1845 in Back Brewery Street,
Cheetham, near Strangeways Brewery and in the shadow of the prison. His
parents, Ira and Margaret Horridge were respectable and hardworking; Ira
was a whitesmith, who made fenders for trains. Robert was the eldest of nine
children: four boys and five girls. The family grew up in the Rochdale Road
area, not far from Smithfield Market. An industrial district with dye works,
engineering works, factories and mills, it was on the edge of Angel Meadow,
a sordid inner-city rookery. The Horridge children attended school and
seemed to have had an ordinary upbringing although, according to Caminada,
Robert showed signs of unusual depravity early on. After leaving school he
became a blacksmith like his father, a trade at which he excelled: 'he was a
first class workman, and a better man at his trade – the fire and anvil – could
not be found, as he could do half as much work again as any other smith in
the country'. But Horridge had barely left his childhood when he turned his
skills and determination to less worthy pursuits and in 1862, aged 16, he was
convicted of stealing money and sentenced to six months in prison.

A capable businessman, Horridge returned to his legitimate occupation
as blacksmith several times during his adult life. He was also a talented
boxer always ready to take on an opponent in the ring. His intelligence,

determination and physical fitness combined, he had the potential for a successful career, like Caminada, if only he had been able to resist the lure of criminal activity.

On 26 March 1866, aged 19, he married Jane Buckley, the daughter of a local carder; at the time Jane was three months pregnant. Robert was 5 feet 7 inches tall, with a fresh complexion, dark brown hair and blue eyes. His skin was covered in pockmarks and his hands were scarred from fighting: this was a man with a history of violence and a dangerous temper. Inevitably, this did not bode well for the marriage and just six months after the wedding, by which time their child had been born, Horridge was convicted of assaulting his wife and sentenced to three months in Belle Vue Prison.

After this stretch in prison, Horridge did not stay at liberty for long. The following year he conspired with 16-year-old John Doran to rob Doran's employer, rival blacksmith James Collinge, of 72 pokers and 60 iron bars. As it was Doran's first offence he received a sentence of just two months. Older and more experienced, Horridge served 18 months at Her Majesty's Pleasure for receiving the stolen goods, leaving his wife and their two children to fend for themselves. Yet, on his release, Horridge returned to his trade as a blacksmith and was successful enough to buy his own business. He even took on a partner: a reliable and industrious Italian called Stephen Fignona, known as 'Ned', who had previously worked for a telegraph company and had a useful sideline as a 'fence', selling on stolen goods.

When Bob Horridge met PC Caminada in 1870, the two men had much in common. Born within a year of one another, they both came from large families and grew up in the slums. As sons of craftsmen, they each received a basic education and enjoyed a reasonably stable childhood. Although Caminada's life became more precarious as his family circumstances declined during his teenage years, it was Horridge who turned to crime. With similar backgrounds, but having made different choices as adults, the pair would meet at pivotal points throughout their lives.

Their rivalry began after Horridge stole a watch from Samuel Mould, near the railway station during Caminada's first year on the beat. A watchmaker identified the stolen watch by a piece missing from the dial, which had been chipped off with a knife. Horridge had left it with him for repair and the following morning when the thief arrived to collect the watch, Caminada was waiting for him. Horridge received a sentence of seven years' penal servitude because of his previous convictions. As he embarked upon his first serious prison sentence, PC Caminada was promoted to Detective Sergeant.

Penal servitude (imprisonment with hard labour) had been introduced in 1853 to replace the practice of transportation for serious offences. The minimum sentence was three years but, unluckily for Horridge, in 1864 it had been increased to five years for a second offence and seven for subsequent convictions. This harsh sentence for a relatively small crime angered Horridge so much that, as he was sent down, he uttered a chilling death threat to the man he held responsible: Detective Caminada.

In 1876, after he had completed his long sentence, Bob Horridge settled back into his home area of Rochdale Road. He re-launched his business, which was even more lucrative than before, possibly due to criminal sidelines, allowing him to buy a pony and cart to convey his goods to warehouses and wholesalers. However, he did not remain straight for long and later that year, he was charged with 'rattening' (damaging) four pairs of bellows belonging to his long-time competitor, blacksmith James Collinge. He was acquitted.

By this time, the police were already aware of Horridge's 'presence' in the city: 'It was very well known that when "Bob" was not in prison robberies occurred more frequently in Manchester than when he was confined'. First a furrier's shop was burgled, then a silk mercer's and a jeweller's. Horridge was the prime suspect, but the police could get no further in their investigation than questioning him about walking home one evening carrying a large hammer.

Bob Horridge was particularly skilled at evading the law and, within a few months of his release, he made the first of a number of daring escapes. On this occasion, he was suspected of a robbery and 20 to 30 police officers surrounded his house in Gould Street, ready to arrest him. When they knocked at the front door, Horridge easily broke his way through the laths and plaster of the ceiling, it being a poorly-constructed tenement, and jumped out onto the roofs of the row of terrace houses. He scampered away across the slates, before slipping down through the roof of a house in a neighbouring street, where he dropped into a bedroom full of sleeping harvest workers, who were too startled to stop him. The police, however, were one step ahead and when Horridge opened the door to leave there were two constables waiting for him on the step. Without the slightest hesitation, he took a flying-leap past the officers and made off down the street.

Horridge's next escapade was in a fancy goods shop. A policeman on his beat spotted him through the shutter, with a companion known as 'Long Dick'. Both men, wearing aprons, were pulling down stock from the shelves. When challenged by the officer Horridge replied, 'It's all right, guv'nor; we're taking stock!' Unconvinced, the policeman slipped round to the back of the premises and found Horridge as he was leaving. The thief struck him a violent blow to the face, knocked him down and made his escape. Long Dick was left to take the fall: he was arrested and sentenced to five years' penal servitude, while Horridge got clean away.

After this close encounter, Horridge laid low for a while. When two officers visited his new home in Addington Street, he again escaped through the ceiling and into an adjoining house. Despite his previous form, it seemed almost impossible to make accusations stick to this skilled and fearless burglar and soon he was up to his old tricks again. This time, he robbed a mill belonging to John Keyner in Bradford, near Manchester. It was the usual practice at the mill to withdraw cash from the bank on Friday evenings to pay the workers' wages on Saturday. Horridge learned that the night watchman left the mill at 4.30am and went to the boiler house to start up the steam, ready for work starting at 6am. In his absence, the watchman took the precaution of locking the door but early one Saturday morning, while he was away from his post, Horridge and three companions, including his former partner in crime, Stephen Fignona, gained entry to the mill by using a false key. They drove a cart up to the mill and loaded it with the safe weighing about 450 lbs and containing £400 in silver and gold.

The gang evaded capture and, three weeks later, following a tip-off, the police found the empty safe in a reservoir behind Horridge's workshop. Although he was prosecuted, once again Bob Horridge was acquitted. Having escaped justice twice in quick succession, Horridge was on a roll and before his criminal career came to an end, there would be more spectacular escapes and burglaries, this time with very grave consequences.

In the summer of 1880 a policeman patrolling in Redfern Street, not far from the cathedral, tried the door of a warehouse, only to discover that it was open. Finding this unusual, he pushed his way in and bumped into Horridge, who was rushing out. Before running off, the thief struck the officer with such violence that he was knocked to the ground. Scrambling to his feet, the policeman was joined in pursuit by a colleague, who was also knocked down after Horridge landed him a heavy blow. Next, a passing journalist tried to stop the fleeing thief and he too was felled. Horridge was out in the open, with no ceilings to escape through, and as the crowd on his heels swelled, he jumped down the steps of the approach to Victoria Railway Station, leaped over the parapet of a footbridge and dived straight into the polluted waters of the River Irk to make his escape.

A few days later, Horridge was apprehended in a local public house and convicted of breaking and entering the warehouse. He received a further seven years' penal servitude, this time in Pentonville Prison. As he was transported to London by rail, he was overheard boasting to the other convicts that it would not be long before he would be free again. The officer in charge forewarned the governor of Pentonville and, when Horridge arrived at the prison, the guards were ready to prevent his escape.

But Horridge stuck to his plan and shortly after, two convicts joined him in a sprint for the wall. The alarm was raised and Horridge's companions surrendered, leaving him alone in his daring escape. A guard fired and the fugitive was wounded, but he carried on running. They shot him twice more before he was forced to surrender. Horridge survived and remained in prison until the end of his sentence when, although now partially paralysed from the injuries sustained in his failed bid for freedom, he was more determined than ever to exact revenge on Chief Inspector Jerome Caminada.

Bob Horridge's final exploit began in the early hours of 30 July 1887, a few days after his release from Pentonville. He and a female accomplice broke into a boot and shoe shop in his old stomping ground of Rochdale Road, using a false set of keys. Luck was against them and PC Bannon, passing by on his regular beat, spotted the pair. Engaging the help of a letter carrier and two other passersby, the officer entered the premises and confronted the burglar. With the bloodcurdling words: 'I will not be taken alive', Horridge fired a gun at PC Bannnon's head. Fortunately the bullet only grazed the policeman's neck. Hearing the commotion, another officer, PC Parkin, came to his colleague's aid and Horridge fired again, shooting him straight in the chest. A passing market cart took the wounded officer straight to the infirmary and, although he survived his dreadful injury, he never fully recovered.

While the double shooting was taking place, Detective Caminada was in Chichester. He was summoned back to Manchester immediately by telegram and arrived later that afternoon. He began his enquiries with the wanted man's family, and Horridge's father and sister informed Caminada that, since Robert's release, he had threatened many times to shoot the detective. Unperturbed, Caminada set out to settle his score with Horridge once and for all.

After discovering that Horridge had fled to Liverpool, Caminada and a colleague disguised themselves as labourers, and travelled by train to the city to track him down. They began their search at the docks, as Horridge's wife had been seen there, and outside the Prince of Wales Public House Inspector Schofield noticed the strange behaviour of a passerby. He commented to his superior officer: 'Did you see that man who has just passed? I saw him look very hard at you'. Caminada turned towards the man and instantly recognised him by his walk as Bob Horridge.

Detective Caminada seized the felon by the arms and greeted him with, 'Hallo! Bob, how are you?' Horridge reached his hand to his trouser pocket, but Caminada drew his revolver and placed the muzzle at full cock to his rival's mouth: 'If there's any nonsense with you, you'll get the contents of this'. The prisoner tried to get his own weapon, but by this time Schofield was on hand and the two policemen fought to restrain him. Caminada struck Horridge on the head with his revolver and they dragged him to the local police station, where he later defended his shooting of the police constables: 'I have had to do what I did, or they would have killed me; it was the officer's own fault he was shot – he would come on to it'. When Caminada searched Horridge he found a loaded six-chambered revolver and a tin box of cartridges: the detective had had a lucky escape.

At the age of 36, Robert Horridge was convicted of attempted murder and sentenced to life imprisonment, remaining in prison until his death. As Caminada concluded:

When Horridge was sent into penal servitude for life the public had the pleasure of knowing that the career of one of the most accomplished and desperate thieves that ever lived in Manchester was brought to an end.

Portrayed in the press as 'a most desperate character', before his life sentence Robert Horridge had spent a total of almost 17 years in prison, but his punishment had not deterred him from his 'career of crime'. This was no surprise to Detective Caminada, who had extensive experience of the penal system and its detrimental effect on criminals.

In the mid-nineteenth century, due to a more organised and increasingly efficient police force, the number of convictions rose steadily and new prisons were built to accommodate them. In 1853 penal servitude started to replace transportation as a form of punishment. Imprisonment with hard labour began with a period of solitary confinement, before the convict was transferred to a public works prison, such as Chatham, Portland, Portsmouth or Dartmoor, to complete their sentence. On their release, ex-convicts were subject to a probationary period of police supervision.

Caminada was scathing in his condemnation of the system:

Penal servitude has become so elaborate that it is now a huge machine for punishment, destitute of discrimination, feeling, or sensitiveness; and its non-success as a deterrent against crime, and its complete failure in reforming criminal character, are owing to its obvious essential tendency to deal with erring human beings – who are still men, despite their crimes – in a manner which mechanically reduces them to the uniform level of disciplined brutes.

Harsh discipline, monotonous routine and mind-numbing physical tasks, such as the treadwheel, shot drill, crank and stone-breaking characterised hard labour in Victorian prisons. Horridge experienced this regime during his two long stretches in the 1870s and 1880s. His first sentence took place at Gillingham All Male Convict Prison in Kent and his second at Pentonville Prison, in North London. Built in 1842, Pentonville was a model British prison. Designed with a central hall and five radiating wings, it was known for the 'separate system', in which prisoners were isolated to prevent 'contamination' of new offenders by seasoned criminals. It became a blueprint for subsequent institutions.

Like Horridge, convicts were transferred from holding prisons for a nine-month period of solitary confinement in Pentonville. Caminada pointed out the flaws of the separate system: 'Notwithstanding all the precautions that may be taken it is impossible to prevent communication between prisoners. An intimacy is formed inside the gaol which is renewed on their discharge, and they are soon back again'. This was certainly the case for Bob Horridge. In Caminada's opinion, the worst criminals were those who had spent the longest time in prison. After extended periods of confinement, they became inured to prison life: 'He loses his self-respect, becomes acquainted with habitual criminals, and goes from bad to worse, until he almost looks upon the gaol as his home'. Outcast from society and with their social networks forged behind bars, on their release hardened criminals like Horridge would turn to their fellow convicts for support.

After Pentonville, Horridge served time in the convict prison on Portsea Island, built in the early 1850s to replace the prison ships, or 'hulks', used to house prisoners waiting for transportation and to ease prison overcrowding. He spent the remaining years of his life sentence in the high-security prison at Parkhurst on the Isle of Wight. After plaguing the city of Manchester for 20 years, Bob Horridge was finally confined for good. Caminada had only arrested him twice, yet the two men seemed to have a connection and a grudging respect for each other, albeit from opposite sides of the law. Perhaps, if Horridge had channelled his energies in a more positive direction, they might have been allies rather than rivals.

Chapter Ten

'City of Martyrs':
Caminada and the Irish Nationalists
(January 1889)

The Irish were right at the bottom of the social and economic pile in Victorian Manchester. Since the early years of the Industrial Revolution there had been a steady flow of migrants from Ireland and arrivals reached a peak in the mid-1840s, during the Great Famine. By the end of the decade, 15 per cent of the city's inhabitants were Irish-born, making them the largest ethnic community. Seeking refuge from poverty and starvation back home, in Manchester they endured the poorest accommodation and lowest paid jobs.

Irish workers settled in the most wretched quarters of the city the worst of which, known as 'Little Ireland', was on the banks of the fetid waters of the River Medlock. A 10-minute walk from Caminada's birthplace, the area was characterised by filthy streets and decrepit housing. When Dr James Kay was commissioned by the Special Board of Health to investigate the district in 1831, he reported that the houses lay so low on the banks of the river that the chimneys could barely be seen above the level of the road:

About two hundred of these habitations are crowded together in an extremely narrow space, and are inhabited by the lowest Irish. Most of these houses have also cellars, whose floor is scarcely elevated above the level of the water flowing in the Medlock. The soughs are destroyed, or out of repair: and these narrow abodes are in consequence always damp, and on the slightest rise of the river, which is a frequent occurrence, are flooded to the depth of several inches.

Some four thousand people struggled to survive in this unhealthy environment. Friedrich Engels referred to it as one of the most miserable places he had ever encountered. The unsanitary back-to-back cottages were set in muddy streets awash with human and animal refuse in stinking puddles of stagnant water from the river, and surrounded by factories belching black smoke into the damp air. Home to between 10 and 20 inhabitants, most houses had just two rooms. There was no running water and the privies were in a disgraceful state with, on average, one toilet for 250 people. In these depressing circumstances the most needy were forced to live in the notorious underground cellar dwellings.

In Manchester, during the 1830s and 1840s, around 20,000 people lived in cellars. Often these were in larger houses, which had declined to a dilapidated state and where the rooms and floors had been partitioned and converted into tenancies. The meanest part of one of these houses was the cellar, which was dark, dank and unhealthy. Cellars were almost subterranean, possessing no ventilation, with little natural light and constant damp. Engels described one cellar, where every day the inhabitant, a weaver, had to empty out the river water that had seeped in during the night. These cellars, about 9 to 10 feet square, were usually inhabited by at least 10 people, often two families, and sometimes as many as 16, as well as livestock. There were no beds, so people slept on rags, straw or wood shavings; cleanliness was impossible and disease rife.

In the late 1840s Little Ireland was demolished to make way for the building of Oxford Road Railway Station. Although they moved elsewhere, the Irish families in the city remained poor for the rest of the century. Faced with such an inhospitable environment and a powerful undercurrent of anti-Irish prejudice, they formed close-knit communities. Also, wherever they settled they built a church; St Augustine's was opened in Little Ireland in 1820, and Caminada's parents were married there 20 years later. In defiance of hostility from the wider community, the migrants forged their own identity as Irish Catholics, and Manchester became a breeding ground for Irish nationalism and revolution. During the first half of the nineteenth century there were many periods of unrest, but these matters were brought sharply to a head with the tragic death in 1867 of police officer, Sergeant Charlie Brett.

The Irish Republican Brotherhood was founded on St Patrick's Day 1858 with the express aim of making Ireland an independent republic by force of arms. After absorbing other Irish revolutionary groups, they became known as the Fenians. By 1865 there were an estimated 20,000 members in the British Isles, with particularly strong support from the Lancashire Irish. In September 1867, following a failed attack on the garrison at Chester Castle two Fenian leaders, Thomas Kelly and his aide Timothy Deasy, were arrested in Manchester. After an appearance in court they were being transported back to Belle Vue Prison, when their comrades launched a daring rescue, which resulted in the fatal shooting of Sergeant Brett. Three men, William Allen, Michael Larkin and Michael O'Brien, were executed for his murder and remembered by the Irish community as the Manchester Martyrs.

After that fateful day the 'City of Martyrs', as Caminada referred to it, played an important part in Irish politics. When he joined the police force in 1868 fear and suspicion of Fenians was already running high, but it was not until the early 1880s that 'things began to get lively'. On 14 January 1881 a bomb exploded at the Salford Infantry Barracks, blowing down part of the armoury wall and damaging a nearby butcher's shed. Fortunately, the 8th Regiment of Foot was absent at the time, but two bystanders, a seven-year-old boy and a woman were injured in the blast. The child suffered a fractured skull and later died in hospital. When gunpowder was found at the bombsite, the Fenians became the prime suspects.

Prior to the explosion, the Chief Constable had received information about the threat and investigated with his right-hand man, Detective Caminada. It was a very foggy day and the two police officers had set up a watch on the Infantry Barracks, but after seeing nothing unusual they left to take up position at the local Cavalry Barracks, and were still there at 5.20pm when the bomb went off. This action marked the beginning of a dynamite campaign that would inspire terror in Britain for the next five years, as the Fenians targeted public buildings and barracks in major cities.

In the aftermath of the first bombing the national police were on the alert and Caminada shadowed a number of 'suspicious-looking individuals' in Manchester. Among them was Thomas Mooney, an Irish bricklayer. Caminada tailed Mooney and his companion to a cottage in Widnes, Cheshire. Once the suspects had left, the detective interrogated the owner of the house, gleaning important information. Mooney had links with Jeremiah O'Donovan Rossa, a prominent Fenian leader, who orchestrated the early bomb attacks in the dynamite campaign. A short while later, following a tip-off from his informant, Caminada staked out the cottage. The owner's wife and seven children had gone to see a magic lantern show and as soon as they had departed, Caminada positioned himself in the coal cellar under the stairs, crouching on one knee with his revolver at full cock.

Two men arrived at the door and called out the password: 'Sailing Ship!' They were admitted at once and Caminada listened from his hiding place, as they discussed a quantity of powder to be transported to London ready for business on Wednesday 16 March, just a few days away. The 80 pounds of explosives were to be taken in a carpetbag and tin trunk. It soon became evident that the 'business' was the bombing of Mansion House, the residence of the Lord Mayor of London. The Mayor had been planning to hold a banquet on 16 March, but it had been cancelled because of the assassination of Tsar Alexander III. A passing policeman foiled the plot, after noticing a smouldering brown paper package under a window recess of the building. He successfully extinguished the flame and defused the bomb, which was in a steel-reinforced deal box packed with old newspaper and scraps of carpetbag. After this abortive attempt at sabotage, Scotland Yard sent instructions to the Chief Constable of Manchester to arrest Mooney and his accomplice, and once again Chief Inspector Caminada was on their tail. After discovering an address in Paris for the suspects from an imprint on a blotting pad left in the cottage in Widnes, he set off for France.

Once in Paris, Caminada waited outside the house in Place des Deux Ecus, near Les Halles, until he spotted his quarry leaving. After following Mooney for a while, he approached him in the market place, calling out: 'Good morning, Tom, how are you?' Uneasy, Mooney reached for the revolver hidden in his trouser pocket, but the detective walked on without stopping. Later, just as he was preparing to make the arrest, Caminada received a telegram from his Chief Constable. It ordered him not to arrest the suspect, but to meet with detectives from Scotland Yard and confirm Mooney's identity for future reference.

His mission accomplished, Caminada and his colleagues from London made their way together to the railway station ready to come home. As they were travelling, they noticed that the French police were following them in the mistaken belief that the detectives themselves were Fenians. When they arrived at the station, the gendarmes surrounded the British police officers and began to interrogate them in French. During the confusion Detective Caminada slipped out and made his way across the buffers onto the waiting train. As the train left the platform he watched his companions being marched away to the local gendarmerie and by the time the misunderstanding had been cleared up, he was well on his way home. Thomas Mooney evaded arrest and was found drowned in mysterious circumstances in New York nine years later.

The dynamite campaign raged for the next four years. The Fenians succeeded in blowing up Mansion House a year after their first attempt and there were several more explosions in the capital, including Paddington and Westminster Bridge underground stations, the government offices at Whitehall, the offices of *The Times* and even the headquarters of the CID. Bombs were also planted in Chester, Liverpool and Glasgow. Due to the vigilance of Caminada and his colleagues, Manchester was spared any further attempts.

Throughout this period of Fenian activity, Caminada's role was to track suspects and pass on information to the British authorities, rather than to make arrests himself. After his trip to Paris, he travelled to Ireland, America, Germany and Switzerland. Many of the suspects he tailed were later arrested, as the CID and the newly formed Special Irish Branch worked to maintain security and protect the public. After the murder of Lord Cavendish, Chief Secretary for Ireland and Thomas Burke, the Permanent Undersecretary, in Phoenix Park, Dublin in 1882, Caminada tracked one of the suspected murderers, John F. Beggs. He followed Beggs from Manchester to Boston, arriving at his lodgings only to find that Beggs was already on his way back to England. Caminada re-crossed the Atlantic and traced him to Ireland. Once again he was ordered not to arrest Beggs; instead he watched his movements and reported them back to the authorities. After the next spate of London bombings, Beggs returned to America, where he was implicated in, and later acquitted of, the murder of Chicago physician, Dr Patrick Henry Cronin in May 1889.

On another occasion in 1884, Caminada was returning on a cargo ship from active duty in Hamburg, when he followed a suspect onto a ferryboat. As it was midnight when they docked in England, the man invited Caminada to spend the night at his home in London, completely unaware that he was a detective. The man's kindness to a fellow traveller 'subsequently proved of the greatest possible service to the police'.

The final stage of the dynamite conspiracy took place in January 1885, when three more bombs exploded in London: inside the House of Commons; Westminster Hall; and in the Banqueting Room of the Tower of London. These events did not mark the end of Caminada's involvement in Irish politics, and four years later he became embroiled in Ireland's bid for independence yet again. On 29 January 1889 Chief Inspector Caminada arrested a high profile political prisoner, who had escaped from a police court in Ireland. The fugitive was the MP for North East Cork, William O'Brien, a well-known journalist, politician and staunch supporter of Irish Home Rule.

A former member of the Fenian movement, O'Brien had been arrested and imprisoned several times by the British authorities, most notably in Mitchelstown, County Cork, after he had encouraged tenants to resist eviction. When O'Brien refused to appear before the magistrates' court, a protest in support of his actions took place in the town, resulting in the police killing three people and wounding several more. After his arrest, protests against his imprisonment led to a demonstration in Trafalgar Square on 13 November 1887, during which two people died. Known as 'Bloody Sunday', casualties included 200 demonstrators and 112 police officers.

Two years later in January 1889, O'Brien found himself once again in the dock of a police court, in Carrick-on-Suir on charges of conspiracy, but this time he absconded. Towards the end of the same month, rumours began to circulate in Manchester that William O'Brien was going to make an appearance at a meeting in Hulme Town Hall to protest against the Prime Minister, Lord Salisbury. A large crowd gathered to see the 'hero who was defying the British government'. The Royal Irish Constabulary had given Detective Caminada a warrant for his arrest and the stakes were high as he set out for Hulme with his officers amid threats of bloodshed, if he dared to apprehend the runaway MP.

When the police arrived at the hall a rough and noisy crowd had already congregated at the gates and the nearby streets were occupied by 'thousands of fiery spirits, who seemed more inclined for a row than a lecture'. Determined to carry out his important duty, Caminada moved into action, placing undercover officers in the audience to gain any snippets of valuable information. At 7.30pm a great cheer rose as a cab drew up and O'Brien was hustled into the hall. Leaning on a hose-cart in the yard, Caminada watched some 300 people rush through the gates behind the politician, who was surrounded by bodyguards.

Inside the hall, the detective went down to the basement and sent word to his Chief Constable that as 'things were looking black', they should send for reinforcements. Within 20 minutes, more than 400 officers had arrived and they moved to block every exit. Caminada was then seized by two of O'Brien's bodyguards: 'I received a good kicking, of which my shins bore the marks for many a day'. All negotiations failed and the Chief Constable sanctioned the meeting to go ahead. After checking that there were no ladders for O'Brien to escape through the windows, Caminada joined his colleagues in the hall, where the rowdy audience jeered at him. While he maintained the public's attention, other officers rounded up the bodyguards and secured the corridors and stairways, sealing all means of escape.

William O'Brien took the stage 'amidst a tempest of applause', as his supporters rose to their feet cheering his name and waving their handkerchiefs, and only quietening down to listen to their hero. At the end of his speech pandemonium broke out, as the audience clambered over reporters' tables and flung chairs out of the way, trying to climb onto the platform to shake the MP's hand. Detective Caminada and the Chief Constable also mounted the stage, but the latter was struck in the chest and pitched back into the screaming crowd. After striking the Chief Constable's assailant a violent blow to the head, Caminada made his way over to O'Brien, who was so jostled by well-wishers that he was on the verge of passing out. Once he had been revived by a glass of water, Caminada helped him clamber off the stage back into the anteroom, while his officers cleared the hall.

There was a tremendous crush but everyone left the room safely, with only one woman carried out in a faint. Pale and worn after being mobbed by his fervent supporters but remaining firm, William O'Brien surrendered to the police without further ado. Outside the venue the angry crowd had swelled to enormous proportions with several hundred demonstrators carrying torches, but despite this the police successfully escorted the escaped prisoner back to Manchester Town Hall.

The following morning, after he had taken breakfast with the mayor and mayoress, four detectives, including Chief Inspector Caminada, escorted O'Brien in secret to Ordsall Lane Station. The 9.40 Dublin Express made an unscheduled stop to pick up the party, and O'Brien travelled in a first class compartment to Holyhead and then by steamer onto Ireland. During the journey Caminada discovered that he was 'a pleasant and agreeable man' and they exchanged stories of their experiences. They parted company at Kingstown and the MP boarded his train for Dublin. Before he left the platform he beckoned Caminada to the window of his carriage and publicly thanked him and the rest of the Manchester Police Force for their kindness.

A devout Catholic, Jerome Caminada did not otherwise seem to have a strong Irish identity, in spite of the fact that the families of both his mother and wife had come from Ireland. He did not grow up in the Irish quarters of Manchester, although the church and school he attended would have had a strong Irish contingent. On the other hand, he never showed any prejudice towards the Irish, which would have been common in his professional circles. Furthermore, the Irish were firmly opposed to the police and the local authorities, placing Detective Caminada in an ambiguous position as a high-ranking officer with Irish origins.

Above all, Caminada was a policeman, and the resolute sense of civic duty that guided his decisions and behaviour makes it less surprising that he acted on behalf of the British authorities, rather than supporting his fellow countrymen in their fight for independence. Towards the end of his career he was accused of being partial towards the Catholic Church and his response encapsulated the motivation to do his duty: 'When an officer is ordered by his superior to do a certain work, it is not his place "to reason why," but to obey orders, otherwise discipline would be at an end'.

Jerome Caminada was a man who did far more than his duty in his role as a detective. A month after his arrest of William O'Brien, he would embark on another high profile case, one that would bring his remarkable skills to the attention of the nation – and prove him to be a real-life Sherlock Holmes.

Chapter Eleven

The Manchester Cab Mystery
(February 1889)

At 6.30pm on Tuesday 26 February, John Fletcher hailed a cab from the steps of Manchester Cathedral. Slightly inebriated following an afternoon of drinking, the middle-aged paper merchant clambered into the hansom in the company of a young man. A short while later, the cab driver dropped the pair at the Three Arrows Public House nearby on Deansgate, and then waited 20 minutes while they went in for a drink. They each ordered two glasses of bitter, paid for by Fletcher.

The young man quickly downed his and just after 7pm, they set off again, this time in the direction of a private address in Stretford Road, towards Old Trafford. En route the road was blocked by a street procession for Mexican Joe's new Wild West Show, then opening on Oxford Road. The cabman had to walk his horse while the parade passed and as they carried on their journey, a passerby called out to him: 'A young fellow has just jumped out of your cab and run down Cambridge Street'. When the driver stepped down to investigate he found that the near side door of the cab was open. Inside John Fletcher was slouched in the back in a semi-conscious state, with his head resting on the seat in front. His companion had disappeared.

The cabbie lifted the slumped passenger's head, rubbing his ears to rouse him. Slurring his words Fletcher muttered, 'Go away, and leave me alone', so the cab driver shut the door, climbed into his seat and drove towards the city centre. At 7.45pm the cab arrived back at the cathedral, where the cabman enlisted the help of a police constable, who suggested he drive his drunken passenger to Albert Street Police Station. But as Fletcher was now unconscious, the driver decided to take him straight to the Royal Infirmary, where the house surgeon, Mr John Hampden Barker, certified that John Fletcher was dead.

The following morning, the inhabitants of Manchester woke to the disturbing news that a respectable businessman had been found dead inside a cab in questionable circumstances. Already horrified by the recent gruesome murders in London attributed to Jack the Ripper, the public would follow the news with morbid fascination as the 'Manchester Cab Mystery' unfolded. The stakes were high, as confirmed in the *Daily Telegraph*:

> *The knowledge that atrocious criminals – such as the perpetrator of the Whitechapel butcheries, for instance – have succeeded in evading discovery for many months and are still at liberty (in all probability rubbing shoulders with well-conducted and law-abiding persons), is heavily fraught with mortification to the people of a civilised country.*

Confidence in the abilities of the police was then at an all-time low and the general public was in danger of becoming hysterical. A quick resolution of this case was vital, but it was not yet clear whether John Fletcher had really been murdered.

There were no marks of violence on his body and, as he was a habitual gin-drinker, the initial report of the hospital surgeon postulated that he had died of alcohol poisoning. However, John Fletcher had no money or valuables on his person when he arrived at the infirmary, just two empty spectacles cases and a chequebook for the Southport Branch of the Manchester and Salford Bank, which suggested that he had been robbed. This puzzling mystery was placed in the capable hands of Detective Chief Inspector Caminada. Without a crime scene, Caminada began his investigation with the clues and facts that he already possessed, in an attempt to piece together the events that had led up to Fletcher's death. His logical starting point was with the victim.

John Fletcher, 50, was the senior partner in a firm of paper manufacturers whose offices were located in the centre of the city. A wealthy man, he was well-known in commercial circles and especially at the Exchange. By 1889 he had retired from active business leaving the firm under the management of his nephew. Fletcher was also a justice of the peace and had recently been elected a member of Lancashire County Council.

On 26 February, after having packed a case for a stay in Knutsford until the weekend, Fletcher had left his house in the seaside town of Southport to travel into Manchester, where he spent the morning at the company's offices in New Brown Street. At 1pm he took his leave to attend a mill auction at the Mitre Hotel, near the cathedral, where he was seen by several friends and colleagues. They later testified that he had been 'somewhat under the influence of drink', but was 'in full possession of his faculties'. Fletcher made an appointment to meet one of them later that evening at Sinclair's, a popular shellfish restaurant in Victoria Market. He never turned up. At 6pm

Deansgate in central Manchester, a bustling thoroughfare with theatres, shops, drinking dens and brothels.

The existing Free Trade Hall, built in 1853 on St Peter's Fields, the site of the Peterloo Massacre.

Back-to-back houses were common in the slums of nineteenth century Manchester. This house in Back Queen St (now the Lloyd St) was close to the back-to-back where Caminada was born.

A typical worker's dwelling in Southern Street, Manchester. Jerome Caminada, aged 14, lived just two doors away from this house in 1858.

Knott Mill Police Station, the headquarters of A Division, where Police Constable Caminada began his career in 1868.

When Caminada was promoted to the Detective Department he worked at Manchester Town Hall.

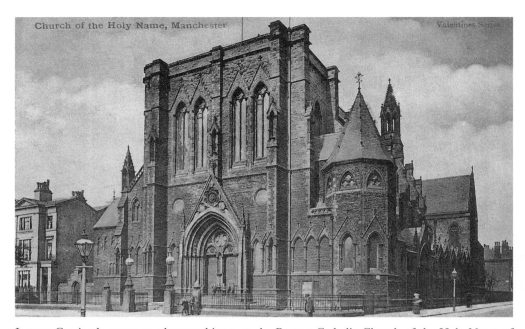

Jerome Caminada was a regular worshipper at the Roman Catholic Church of the Holy Name of Jesus, on Oxford Road.

London Road Railway Station (now Manchester Piccadilly) built in 1842. Railway stations were often the haunts of thieves and pickpockets during this period.

Reverend Edward James Silverton, Baptist minister and quack doctor.

AT THE FREE-TRADE HALL, MANCHESTER, DAILY, NOW, up to Friday, June 6th, at 7 p.m.

REV. E. J. SILVERTON.

Wonderful Cures of

DEAFNESS

And NOISES IN THE HEAD AND EARS,

Affections of the Eyes, Neuralgic Pains, Indigestion, Constipation, Blood Diseases, Kidney and Liver Complaints, Gout and Rheumatism, Bronchitis, Asthma, Consumption, General Weakness and Wasting, and many other Diseases.

CONSULTATIONS FREE DAILY.

from 11 to 1 and 3 to 7.

Rev. E. J. SILVERTON, of London, and his physician are in attendance. Sufferers should take the earliest opportunity of paying them a visit.

Advertisement for daily consultations by Reverend Silverton at the Free Trade Hall placed in the *Manchester Courier and Lancashire General Advertiser*, 22 May 1884.

The front page of the *Illustrated Police News*, 9 October 1880.

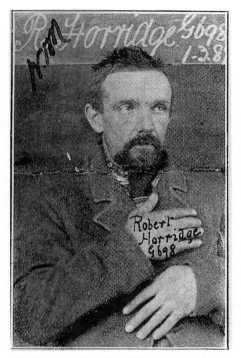

(*Left*) Robert Horridge, blacksmith and violent thief.

(*Right*) Horridge's escape from the house in Gould Street.

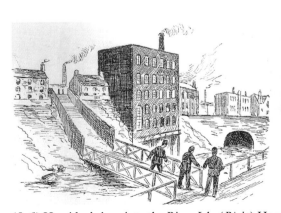

(*Left*) Horridge's leap into the River Irk. (*Right*) Horridge escaping from the warehouse in Redfern Street.

THE MANCHESTER CAB MYSTERY.

MR. FLETCHER.   THE PRISONER, CHAS. PARTON.

Above we give a portrait of Mr. John Fletcher, whose sudden death in a cab has been the cause of a lengthened inquiry both before the Deputy City Coroner, and Mr. F. J. Headlam and the city magistrates at the City Police-court. We also give a portrait of the man Charles Parton, who is charged with causing the death of Mr. Fletcher, as he appeared at the Police-court yesterday.

(*Left*) Paper merchant, John Fletcher, was murdered in a hansom cab in February 1889. (*Right*) Fletcher's killer: 18-year-old Charles Parton, *Manchester Courier and Lancashire General Advertiser*, 9 March 1889.

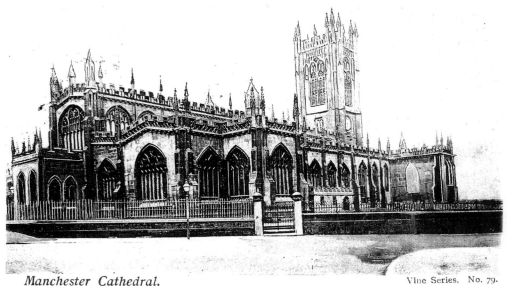

Manchester Cathedral.   Vine Series. No. 79.

John Fletcher hailed a cab on the steps of Manchester Cathedral, unaware that later that evening he would meet his death at the hands of his young companion.

ELIZABETH REMINGTON.

ASHWORTH READ.

Wealthy mill-owner, Ashworth Read, and his lover, Elizabeth Ann Remington, were arrested for the murder of their illegitimate child in 1893, (*Burnley Express and Advertiser*, 7 October, 1893).

Royal Exchange, Manchester.

After his acquittal, Ashworth Read returned to his work and was chased from the trading floor of the Royal Exchange.

DR. W. J. HESLOP,
POLICE SURGEON.

CHIEF COURT INSPECTOR
MASON.

E. 1.

Young offenders (under 14) were often sentenced to corporal punishment: birching or flogging.

Detective Caminada supported the use of corporal punishment rather than long prison sentences.

Greengate in Salford was the territory of the infamous Greengate scuttlers. Constable Caminada was attacked there whilst trying to break up a gang-fight.

THE ANARCHISTS AND ARDWICK GREEN!

OBSTRUCTION OR OPPRESSION?

The City Council uphold Perjury and Violence.

OVERTURES OF PEACE REJECTED.

Caminada authorized to break the Heads of Manchester Citizens.

This Tyranny shall not succeed!

The ANARCHISTS will be at ARDWICK GREEN on SUNDAY NEXT, OCTR. 29, at 11-30.

An Indignation Meeting will be held in Stevenson Square at 3.

ATTEND IN YOUR THOUSANDS!

The Manchester Anarchist Group campaigned for freedom of speech at Ardwick Green, 1893.

(Image reproduced with kind permission of the Greater Manchester Police Museum and Archives)

Official photograph of Jerome Caminada, late 1890s. (Image reproduced with kind permission of the Greater Manchester Police Museum and Archives)

JOE THE POSTMAN. WALTER GRIFFITHS LLOYD.

DETECTIVE SERGEANT HARRIS. PAYMASTER SERGEANT. DETECTIVE SERGEANT WILSON.

Caminada's colleagues in E Division.

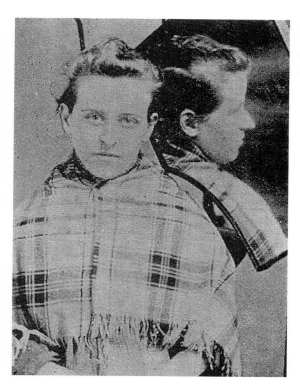

A third of the criminals arrested in Victorian Manchester were female and Caminada encountered many wayward women in his daily work.

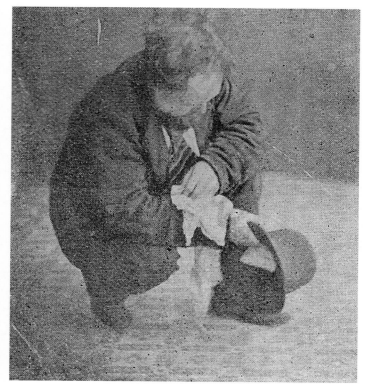

Travelling thieves and beggars plagued the city, but Detective Caminada knew all their ruses.

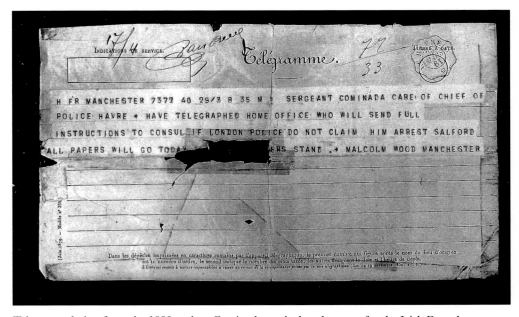

Telegrams dating from the 1880s, when Caminada worked undercover for the Irish Branch.
(Images reproduced with kind permission of the Greater Manchester Police Museum and Archives)

Election poster for Caminada's candidature for Openshaw Ward, 1907.

MUNICIPAL ELECTION, 1907.

OPENSHAW WARD.

VOTE FOR CAMINADA,

THE PRACTICAL MAN.

Your Friend and Neighbour.

Printed and Published by Duckworth & Schofield, Openshaw.

VOTE FOR CAMINADA

The Strong Opponent of Atheism and disastrous Socialism.

VOTE FOR CAMINADA

The old Trade Unionist, who is so thoroughly conversant with Openshaw and Manchester.

The Candidature of

Mr. JEROME CAMINADA

is heartily approved of by the

Manchester Ratepayers' Association.

OPENSHAW WARD.

Municipal Election, 1910.

LADIES & GENTLEMAN,

At the request of a large and influential body of Ratepayers in this Ward, I have again consented to stand for Election as your Representative in the City Council on November 1st.

During the three years that I have been in the Council I have attended faithfully to your interests. From the time I entered the Council to September 3rd of this year I HAD ATTENDED 1149 COUNCIL AND COMMITTEE MEETINGS AND HAVE ONLY BEEN ABSENT ON 25 OCCASIONS. I am responsible for the provision of MUSIC IN THE OPENSHAW RECREATION GROUND on the same lines that it is provided in the Public Parks. I am also responsible for the additional NEW BOWLING GREEN AT DRUMMERS STREET RECREATION GROUND, for the installation of an aerating plant at Whitworth Baths and for the IMPROVED LIGHTING AND PAVING of many streets in the Openshaw Ward.

I have always endeavoured to give careful ATTENTION TO ANY COMPLAINTS which residents in the Ward have made to me.

I am a Member of the Executive Committee of the Manchester Ratepayers Association, in the work of which I take a great interest. I am also Chairman of the Manchester, Salford & District Property Owners Association.

I am opposed to the excessive Officialism which still exists in Municipal Affairs.

I am a strong advocate for LOWER RATES, and also for their EQUALISATION.

I am in favour of Municipal CONTRACTS being given to local firms paying the STANDARD RATE OF WAGES whenever practicable.

I am in favour of REDUCED TRAM FARES FOR WORKERS, and have always supported any measures which had this for its object.

I am opposed to the Extension of Municipal Trading, as it unfairly competes with established firms, and involves dearer and less efficient work than is obtained through Public Tender.

I am strongly OPPOSED TO SOCIALISM as at present understood, and equally strongly opposed to the Atheism openly advocated by many leading writers and speakers of the Socialist Party.

If again returned as your Representative I am prepared to take my Mandate from the Electors of Openshaw and to STUDY THEIR INTERESTS on all occasions.

Thanking you for your confidence during the past three years, and hoping to be again favoured with it,

I am, Ladies and Gentlemen,

Your Obedient Servant,

JEROME CAMINADA.

2, Denmark Rd., C-on-M.,
October 7th 1910

(*Left*) Handbills for Caminada's Manchester City Council elections, 1907. (*Right*) Caminada's manifesto for re-election to the Council in 1910.

SUFFER THE LITTLE CHILDREN
TO COME UNTO ME, AND FORBID THEM NOT,
FOR OF SUCH IS THE KINGDOM OF HEAVEN.
MARK 10 - 14

LOUIS CAMINADA
BORN APRIL 24TH 1883, DIED JULY 8TH 1884

MARY AMELIA CAMINADA
BORN APRIL 9TH 1885, DIED MAY 17TH 1885

CHARLES CAMINADA
BORN SEPT 4TH 1886, DIED DECR 25TH 1886

MARY CAMINADA
DIED AUGUST 27TH 1895, AGED 83 YEARS

MARY WAINHOUSE
DIED FEBRUARY 26TH 1901, AGED 78 YEARS
"MAY THEY REST IN PEACE"

JEROME CAMINADA
DIED MARCH 10TH 1914, AGED 70 YEARS

ALSO AMELIA HIS WIFE
DIED AUG. 23RD 1928, AGED 73 YEARS

(*Above*) Whitworth Park, opposite the home of Jerome Caminada in the early 1900s. (*Left*) The Caminada family grave in Southern Cemetery, Manchester.

a police officer spotted Fletcher at a market stall, accompanied by a young man.

PC William Jakeman described Fletcher's companion as about 22 years old, 5 feet 2 inches tall, with a fresh, clean-shaven complexion. He was wearing a dark brown suit and a chimney-pot hat. The officer added that Fletcher's own clothes had been 'slightly disarranged'. Shortly after this sighting, the two men flagged down the cab, in which the businessman would meet his death less than an hour later. The cabman, Henry Goulding, confirmed that he had taken Fletcher and his acquaintance to the Three Arrows Public House and then to the cathedral to avoid the procession. His description of the suspect concurred with that of the policeman: the young man was about 5 feet 3 inches tall, clean shaven with a fresh face and wearing a brown suit, a watch guard and a felt hat.

During his initial enquiries Caminada discovered that Fletcher had been wearing a pair of gold-rimmed spectacles and an expensive gold watch worth £120. He had also been carrying a purse containing gold sovereigns, all of which had disappeared by the time his body reached the hospital. All the signs indicated that he had been murdered during an attempted robbery and a picture of the possible killer was starting to emerge, but there was still no medical evidence to corroborate Caminada's theory.

Meanwhile, the first inquest into Fletcher's death took place at the coroner's court on 1 March. The landlady of the Three Arrows attested that she had spoken to the deceased in the company of a young man at about a quarter to seven on the night in question, but she could not give a description of either of them or confirm that Fletcher had been wearing a gold watch. As none of the other witnesses had any substantial information to add, the deputy coroner adjourned the inquest until 4 March while the city analyst, Charles Estcourt, examined the contents of the victim's stomach. It was still possible that John Fletcher had died of natural causes but, convinced that a murder had taken place, Detective Caminada redoubled his efforts to find the killer.

The day after the inquest, *The Blackburn Standard* reported that the investigation into the missing companion of John Fletcher was 'not very promising', and that the police had 'made very slight progress'. But behind the scenes, Chief Inspector Caminada had been working hard and had already ruled out the address in Stretford Road, to which the cabman had been taking the two men: it was a lock-up shop belonging to a tailor, who had no knowledge of the victim. Next he found the passerby who had alerted the cab driver to his absconding passenger. The witness had been standing by Lipton's shop and as the cab drove past he had seen a hand reach out of the window to open the carriage door. He then watched, as the man dropped off the step and ran down a footpath towards All Saints Church on Oxford Road.

With the fresh information Caminada visited the neighbourhood to see if his prime suspect had left a trail. Sure enough he learned that a young man fitting the witnesses' description had been seen in a beerhouse called the York Minster, near High Chatham Street. The man, wearing a dark brown check waistcoat with a valuable gold watch and chain, had ordered a glass of soda water and milk and then asked the landlord, James Holden, for some change, pulling out a handful of gold and silver coins. Saying in passing that he was a stranger in town from London, when he had finished his drink, around 8.25pm, he hailed another cab outside the tavern.

Confident that he was on the right track, Caminada located the second cabman who had driven the suspect away from the York Minster to another public house, the Locomotive Inn, on the other side of the cathedral. The cabman, William Coleman, gave details of the watch and guard that the young man had been wearing, which corresponded to the one belonging to John Fletcher. He reported that the suspect had ridden on the box with him and even asked to drive the horse, but after a while he began to shiver with the cold and climbed inside the carriage. In spite of these promising developments, Caminada still could not prove that a crime had been committed and even if it had, he did not have a shred of concrete evidence. He would need the brilliant powers of deduction of Sherlock Holmes to solve this baffling mystery.

The Locomotive Inn was noted for pugilists, so Caminada deduced that his suspect might have had a connection with illegal fighting contests. Relying on his encyclopaedic knowledge of the pugilistic fraternity, he compared the description of his suspect with all likely candidates and the son of a fighter, Charlie Parton, instantly came to mind. His father, John Parton, nicknamed 'Pig Jack' because of his previous trade as an iron dealer, had run a beerhouse in Greengate, a run-down quarter of the neighbouring city of Salford. The tavern had been the haunt of fighters, racecourse thieves and other ne'er-do-wells.

Most importantly, it was rumoured that John Parton used to drug customers by adding a noxious substance to their beer, so that it was easier to rob them. He even drugged the water used for washing out the mouths of the opponents of the men he had backed in the prizefights. All Caminada's instincts told him that he had at last found a positive lead: 'The more I thought of the matter, the more I felt convinced that I was on the right track and at length I determined to arrest him'.

Eighteen-year-old Charles Parton was living with his parents not far from the Locomotive Inn. At 12.30am on 2 March, four days after John Fletcher's death, the suspect was at home in his bed when the detective and his officers raided the house and arrested him. The next morning, several witnesses including the two cabmen and PC Jakeman, picked out Parton as the young companion of John Fletcher in an identity parade. In his defence Parton contended that he had been at a greyhound race in his home city of Liverpool at the time of the alleged crime; the case would hinge on this seemingly insignificant detail. Caminada charged him with having stolen the watch and a sum of money from the deceased businessman and Parton was brought before the stipendiary magistrate, who remanded him in custody pending further enquiries.

Prior to the death of John Fletcher, the Manchester Detective Office had received a communication from their colleagues in Liverpool about a young man wanted for the theft of a bottle of chloral hydrate. Caminada had a hunch that these two crimes were connected:

Then I was strongly impressed by the fact that the prisoner, Charles Parton, said that he had been at a coursing meeting in the neighbourhood of Liverpool, and should he be the offender, there would at once be an explanation of his possession of the poison.

Without further delay, the detective set off to Liverpool to interview the druggist from whom the chemical had been stolen.

On 19 February, a young man had entered Charles Bromley's chemist shop and asked for 40 grains of chloral for his mother, who suffered from angina. When the chemist refused to give him the substance without a prescription, the customer had requested a smaller amount of 10 grains. Bromley had agreed and, as he was weighing the chloral hydrate, the man leaned over the counter, snatched the bottle, which contained about a pound of the substance, and ran out of the shop. The description of the thief confirmed to Caminada that his suspicion was correct.

Whilst Caminada was pursuing his own line of enquiry, two other matters came to light that would have a significant impact on the case. The first startling revelation was the statement of a grocer from Ancoats called Samuel Oldfield. On the evening of 8 January 1889, Oldfield had been out drinking with some friends in a beerhouse near the marketplace in Manchester. At 10.30pm they had left the tavern and met up with another acquaintance near Victoria Railway Station, who had persuaded them to join him and his companion in one last drink. The following morning Oldfield woke up in a police cell with no recollection of the night before. Even though the police had considered him to have been drunk, when Oldfield discovered that his watch and money were missing he suspected that he might have been drugged. Now, almost two months later, he came to the detective office and identified Parton as the 'companion' responsible for the robbery and attempted poisoning.

As interest in the case increased, more information came forth. A second incriminating incident had taken place on 28 December of the previous year when John Parkey, a railway porter from Ashton–under–Lyne, had undergone a similar experience to that of Oldfield the grocer. He had come to Manchester for a festive drink with a friend at the Wheatsheaf Hotel, near Smithfield Market. At the end of the evening they had been on their way to London Road Railway Station when they bumped into Parton and his brother coming out of the White Bear in Piccadilly. Parkey's friend knew Parton's brother and so all four went into a nearby public house for a drink. As the beer flowed Parkey and Parton began to quarrel about boxing and the latter asked the others if they could leave them alone to sort it out. When the other men returned they found Parkey in a state of stupor with Parton helping him into a cab. The next morning he discovered that he had been robbed of his watch and money. A pattern was forming with Charles Parton right at the centre, but Caminada knew that a successful conviction for murder would rely on conclusive proof of poisoning.

When the first official medical evidence was presented at the city police court on 8 March, every available seat in the lower gallery was taken and even the standing room in the upper gallery was full of spectators, who would have to remain on their feet for the next five and a half hours. At 11pm the prisoner, Charles Parton, entered the dock, where he sat down and gazed out at the spectators. Before the stipendiary magistrate, Mr F. J. Headlam, the charges were read out against Parton: the murder of John Fletcher; the theft from him of a gold watch and chain; the administering of chloral to the victim for the purpose of robbery; as well as the two counts of robbery in the earlier cases of Parkey and Oldfield. As the proceedings got under way Parton paid keen attention and conversed frequently with his solicitor.

The public listened with bated breath as the medical report was delivered. All the experts agreed that John Fletcher's death was caused by 'syncope', or loss of consciousness, but the key issue was whether alcohol, chloral hydrate, or a combination of both, had caused his fatal collapse. That Fletcher was a habitual drinker was never in doubt: John Robert Fletcher testified that his uncle had suffered from heart disease and occasionally got intoxicated. When his body had arrived at the Royal Infirmary, the house surgeon had assumed that he had died of alcohol poisoning. This assessment was supported by the fact that during the post-mortem examination, Fletcher's body parts had smelled strongly of alcohol. In addition the deceased's liver was deemed to be a 'gin drinker's liver', although this was at an early stage and was not considered to have contributed fully to his death.

Dr Ernest Septimus Reynolds, resident medical officer at the infirmary, who had assisted with the post-mortem examination, described Fletcher as: 'a bullnecked man, who had undoubtedly consumed a vast amount of ardent spirits'. He added that if John Fletcher had taken chloral for insomnia for three to four months, then it could have contributed to his untimely death. As neither doctor could rule out the possibility that the victim had died of alcohol poisoning, his stomach and intestines had been sent to Charles Estcourt, the city analyst, to test for traces of chloral hydrate.

In the first ever case of a criminal prosecution for chloral hydrate poisoning in Britain, Mr Estcourt received three sealed jars from the deputy coroner, containing Fletcher's body parts and, undertaking 'a delicate test', he found traces of chloral in two of them; it was difficult to detect any evidence of the substance in the stomach, as the chemical is soluble. The amount of chloral present in the body was also unclear. In recorded cases of accidental poisoning, 20 grains of chloral was the smallest dose known to kill a human being, yet 160 grains had also been ingested without resulting in death. However, chloral is far more dangerous when taken with alcohol. Although the medical evidence was inconclusive, Parton was committed for trial at the Liverpool Assizes on the charge of wilful murder. It was during this interval between the committal and the trial that Caminada would play his final card.

Between the court hearings, the detective learned from his network of informants that there had been another key witness in the Three Arrows on 26 February, who could prove without a shadow of a doubt that Parton had drugged John Fletcher. Although he was initially reluctant to get involved in the case, Caminada persuaded Edward Phillips, a bookkeeper in a local firm, to give a statement in which he revealed that he had seen the two men in conversation on that night. In another twist in this astonishing case, Phillips admitted that he had witnessed the prisoner pour a liquid from a small phial into the deceased's beer. He justified his earlier silence by professing that he had presumed it was medicine and only after the extensive coverage in the press had he realised that he was an eyewitness to murder.

At 10.30am on Monday 18 March, almost exactly three weeks after the death of John Fletcher, the murder trial of Charles Parton began at St George's Hall, Liverpool. Earlier that morning there had been so many people waiting on the steps of the Crown Court to watch the trial that the doors had been under threat of being pushed open. The press commented on the surprising number of ladies present in court.

After entering a plea of 'Not guilty', the prisoner maintained an air of calmness as the courtroom drama played out before him. All the details of the case were covered, including the testimony of the bookkeeper and the additional information that Parton's father, 'Pig Jack', had been treated for angina, thus strengthening the link with the theft of chloral hydrate from the chemist. When the thorny question of the medical evidence was broached, Charles Estcourt confirmed that he had found traces of chloral hydrate in the deceased's stomach and intestines. Professor of Pathology, Dr Julius Dreschfeld, gave evidence that he had examined the heart, kidneys and liver of the victim and had concluded that death was caused by the combined effect of alcohol and chloral.

Just after noon on the second day of the trial, Mr Justice Charles gave his summary and the jury retired to consider their verdict. Twenty minutes later, they returned to the courtroom with a unanimous verdict of 'Guilty' and a recommendation for mercy on account of the defendant's youth. The ladies in the public gallery sobbed and Parton clutched the front rail of the dock, as the judge donned his black cap and passed the death sentence.

The sensational climax of the Manchester Cab Mystery, also known as 'The Mystery of a Four-Wheeled Cab', was widely reported in the local and national newspapers. As stated in the *Daily Telegraph*, confidence in the police had been restored after the fear instilled in the general public by the 'Whitechapel butcheries'. The *Manchester Courier* also praised the investigation:

Great credit is due to the Chief Constable of Manchester and to his excellent lieutenant, Chief Detective-Inspector Caminada, for the thoroughness with which they had succeeded in unravelling what, at that time, was regarded as a serious outrage.

Soon after the watch committee increased Chief Inspector Caminada's salary from £200 to £250 per annum.

On 23 March the *Lancaster Gazette* printed a short article apparently containing the confession of the murderer. It reported that while Parton had been held at Manchester Town Hall, an acquaintance of his father had visited him in the cells and the prisoner had given a full confession. It was alleged that Parton, referring to the administration of the drug, had said, 'I gave him more than I intended, and when we came out of the Three Arrows I saw he was a "gonner", so I put him in the cab and got away as soon as I could'. The dubious confession was never passed on to the police.

There was no doubt that Charles Parton was guilty of this heinous crime but, maybe influenced by the *Lancaster Gazette* confession, the people of Manchester were keen to save him from the gallows and soon after the sentencing his barrister initiated a petition to the Home Secretary for a commutation of the death penalty. The request was granted and Parton's sentence reduced to penal servitude for life. A year later Parton's actions claimed the life of a second victim, when John Parkey succumbed to the lingering illness that he had suffered from since being drugged.

Although Detective Caminada was not a 'first-class chemist' like Sherlock Holmes, his solving of the Manchester Cab Mystery in record time was undoubtedly his finest moment and perhaps the pinnacle of his illustrious career. It was the case with which he would be most closely associated and, according the *Manchester Courier*, 'placed him in the foremost rank of the detectives in his day'.

Chapter Twelve

The Beautiful Crook
(1890–1891)

*To Sherlock Holmes she is always the woman. I have seldom heard him
mention her under any other name. In his eyes she eclipses and predominates
the whole of her sex.*
(Sir Arthur Conan Doyle, A Scandal in Bohemia, 1891)

The infamous adventuress of the Sherlock Holmes novels, Irene Adler,
is beautiful, intelligent, resolute and above all, a consummate forger and
blackmailer. While Sir Arthur Conan Doyle was writing about Holmes's
first meeting with her, Detective Caminada was tackling a real-life Irene
Adler, who bore many striking similarities to her fictional counterpart.

In March 1890 an advertisement appeared in a Manchester newspaper for
a loan of £300 requested by a lady with security in the form of an inheritance
of £11,000 (equivalent to almost a million pounds today). The 'lady' was
Alicia Anna Harris Ormonde aged 25, a well-educated woman with an
aristocratic background and expensive tastes, including a penchant for
drinking Madeira with dinner. She was also an experienced crook: an expert
swindler, who was 'one of the most skilful in her profession' and wanted in
various parts of the country for a string of offences. As soon as the police
were on her tail, Alicia would disappear again without trace. A highly skilled
forger, she employed aliases and disguises to hoodwink her victims, who
were usually moneylenders. She was particularly adept at imitating other
people's handwriting, which she put to good use forging legal documents
and letters to elicit money from her many lovers.

When it became apparent that this seductive swindler had taken up
residence in Manchester, the case was assigned to Chief Inspector Caminada,
who began his investigation by searching out one of Alicia's victims. The
detective soon located a moneylender who had answered the request for the
loan. Mr T. Alker, a financial agent with offices in Manchester city centre,
had requested to meet the potential borrower before making the necessary
arrangements for the transaction. At the meeting Alicia Ormonde had

explained that she was still waiting for the inheritance from her late mother and produced a copy of her mother's will as proof, in addition to a reference from her solicitor in Market Harborough. After she signed the forms agreeing to the terms of the repayment, Alker had written to the solicitor for a further guarantee, from whom he had received a favourable reply. The paperwork was completed and Alker was ready to hand over the cash.

However, the evening before the transaction was due to take place, Caminada arrested Ormonde near Manchester Cathedral. On meeting her for the first time, he was captivated:

Our adventuress was young, beautiful, and lady-like. She had a good carriage, and understood all the shifts and expedients, however singular and ingenious, to which the female aspirant for fashion has recourse.

In her pocket he found a draft copy in pencil of the fake letter from her solicitor to Alker and several copies of the phony will.

Despite her airs and graces, Alicia Anna Harris Ormonde was the daughter of a labourer in Leicestershire. She had forged the will, the letters and the legal documents. Caminada succeeded in securing her conviction for fraud and three other charges of theft, even though her infatuated victims were reluctant to testify against her. The 'lady of many aliases' was sentenced to 12 months' imprisonment. On her release she took up her 'position' again and served a further 12 months in Birmingham during 1892.

In *A Scandal in Bohemia*, 'the best plans of Mr Sherlock Holmes were beaten by a woman's wit'. In fact, Irene Adler was the only woman in whom the consulting detective showed any interest, perhaps because she outwitted him. In real life Detective Caminada came across many duplicitous women and Alicia Ormonde was not the only sham heiress that he encountered. Soon after, he met another woman who also used her charms to procure money from gullible men.

When Elizabeth Margaret Burch resorted to subterfuge to save her sisters from financial ruin, the act would start her on a lifetime of crime. Her sisters, Augustine and Zara Burch, were court dressmakers. They had set up a business in Kensington with a capital of £400, but after three years they went bankrupt. Their charitable sister, Elizabeth, stepped in and raised enough cash to pay off their debts.

Elizabeth Burch, 39, was able to help her sisters because she had recently become a wealthy heiress. The circumstances of her unexpected inheritance were widely reported in the press. In May 1888 Burch, who was living in South Kensington, had been among a crowd gathered in St James's Park to watch the arrival of ladies to Buckingham Palace, when an elderly gentleman had fainted. She helped him to a seat in the park and sent an errand boy for a cup of water to revive him. The grateful gentleman asked for Miss Burch's card before he left for his home in the Midlands. A few years later Elizabeth Burch heard from the gentleman's solicitor that he had died and left his estate to her, as he had no near relatives. The unexpected inheritance amounted to £150,000.

Following the publication of this wonderful news, Miss Burch, who had moved to Ashford, Kent, began to enjoy her new lifestyle by placing orders with local shopkeepers for fine foods and expensive clothes. Receiving many letters of congratulations, as well as the inevitable requests for charitable donations, the newly-made 'Ashford Heiress' used her elevated position to raise money for various charities, notably for the victims of the Sandgate Landslip in Folkestone and a colliery explosion in South Wales. Generous donations came flooding in, but when the supposed inheritance was not forthcoming, Miss Burch's creditors began to pursue her in earnest.

The Ashford Heiress dealt with her problems by changing her name and moving to a different town. She repeated this clever act several times, before ending up in Manchester as 'Lady Russell'. An ingenious con artist, her first port of call was a gentleman's house in Higher Crumpsall, where she stole sheets of headed notepaper. She later used them to forge letters of introduction from this respectable family to gain access into the higher circles of society, ready to re-start her 'charitable' works. However, she had not bargained for the suspicious nature of Chief Inspector Caminada who, as soon as he learned that she was receiving correspondence under a different name, detected an elaborate scam.

When the detective and his colleague visited Lady Russell at her apartment, she was sitting at her writing desk. She explained to the officers that she was a 'lady of means' connected with a titled family and was raising money for the South Wales colliery explosion fund. Caminada noted, 'She was most stylishly attired, and wore a pair of gold-rimmed spectacles'. On searching the property he found letters from donors, some of which arrived with the postman while he was present. He also discovered subscription lists for several charities, such as the National Benevolent Institution and the Aged Pilgrim's Friendly Society, and when he inspected them more closely he saw that she had marked the names, mostly female, of those to whom she had addressed begging letters. Among her private papers, he spotted a memorandum book interleaved with blotting paper and, although she had torn out the pages, the imprint of sums of monies received, ranging from 1s to £5 5s, remained as evidence to her fraudulent activities.

The publicity generated by the case brought forth further evidence of Burch's long career of swindling and she was convicted of obtaining money by false pretences, receiving a sentence of six months' imprisonment with hard labour in Strangeways Prison. She later admitted that the letters were fake, but said that the incident with the elderly gentleman in St James's Park was true, although there had been no subsequent inheritance. During her stay in prison she turned her hand to creative writing and submitted her stories to publishers and to the novelist, James Payn, who was coincidentally Sir Arthur Conan Doyle's patron at the *Cornhill* literary magazine. Although her previous existence had been a work of fiction, there is no evidence to suggest that she was as successful in her endeavour to become a writer.

Not all the female criminals that Detective Caminada encountered were beautiful and sophisticated; most of them were far from it. In Victorian Manchester life was hard for women, especially in the rookeries of the city centre. The undercover journalist who investigated the slums for the *Manchester Evening News* in 1874, ran into some pitiful examples in Deansgate: 'The women are of a class whose degradation was utter, and whose reclamation, as a body, is an absolute impossibility'. During his research he met plenty of colourful female characters, with nicknames such as One-Armed Kitty, Cabbage Ann and Ginger Liz – all of whom were well-known to Caminada. Adopting numerous aliases and operating from some of the poorest quarters of the city, these women were thieves, pickpockets and prostitutes.

According to the Manchester Police returns for 1874, 33 per cent of those arrested were female. Crimes typically committed by women included pickpocketing, theft, receiving stolen goods, counterfeiting coins, begging, drunkenness and prostitution. Women often worked as the accomplices of pimps and bullies. They would deceive a passing gentleman into helping them or, less innocently, pose as a prostitute and then take him to a dark corner or narrow alleyway, where with the rest of the gang, she would attack and rob him. If the victim was lucky, he would escape a garrotting. The bold and brutal practice of garrotting was a regular feature of the Mancunian underworld, especially in the early 1860s, when garrotters terrified the public throughout the country. A letter to the *London Standard* summed up the dangers in 1862:

Garrotting has been so common of late that it is absolutely necessary that steps be taken at once to crush its growth… Surely such a state of things cannot be endured. We shall have to arm ourselves to the very teeth or the punishment of these base cowards must be made proportionate to the injury they inflict.

Detective Caminada was accustomed to dealing with such women and their antics were part and parcel of his daily work. Once when he was walking near Victoria Railway Station after dark, a woman tapped him on the shoulder with the words: 'Hello, Sharp Shoes! You haven't got me yet'. It was so dark that Caminada could not see her face, but when they came into the light of a vault, he recognised her as 'Sally', a begging letter writer often seen outside the station asking for money to take her sick child to the Clinical Hospital in London. In a good mood that evening, she set the detective a challenge to arrest her. Caminada rose to the bait: 'Well, I'll start from tonight, and see how long it will take me'.

It did not take him long at all. During the same week he was at the house of the mayor, when the mayor's wife told him about a woman who had been pestering them with begging letters. The detective knew immediately that the culprit was Sally, so he arrested her that evening. She was charged with four cases of begging and received a 12-month prison sentence. After that she gave Detective Caminada a wide berth.

Street begging was endemic on the streets of Manchester and Caminada had little time for professional beggars, as he suspected that most of those in genuine need were too proud to cadge from strangers. Although he had compassion and sympathy for the needy, he believed from experience that giving alms when importuned in public, was often misguided and a real dilemma for passersby:

It can never be a matter of indifference whether money given to the poor is given rightly or wrongly; it either does a great deal of good, or a great deal of harm. Given to one person it may tide him over a moment of difficulty, and rescue him from hopeless beggary; given to another, it merely supplies him with the means of spending one more night in the gin-shop, and encourages his neighbours to do the like.

On one occasion Caminada was patrolling Oxford Street, when he encountered a regular street beggar known as 'Soldier Mary Ann'. Stationed near the Prince's Theatre with a child in her arms under a shawl, she reached out to well-dressed theatregoers for a few coins. Having gained their attention she would follow gentlemen for a few yards, recounting her sorrowful tale of having been abandoned by her husband who was in the army, until they handed over some money. Caminada engaged her in conversation and as she regaled him with her usual patter, he noticed that she kept putting her hand inside the shawl, as if to make breathing space for the child.

Uncomfortable with challenging a beggar who might be in genuine need, he walked on ahead of her to watch what she did. As soon as his back was turned, Mary Ann fled down the street, dropping the baby as she ran. The infant turned out to be a 'good, big lad', who also took to his heels. Caminada gave chase and handing Mary Ann over to the custody of two onlookers, he followed the lad to his home where he discovered that his parents hired him out for three pence a night. As there was no law against irresponsible parenting, Caminada had to content himself with giving them a stern lecture.

'Soldier Mary Ann', whose real name was Ann Ryan, was found guilty of begging and received a sentence of 12 months. Following her release, Caminada came across her once again in equally dubious circumstances. He had been walking in Salford, when he saw two women with bulky packages under their skirts. He followed them home to Fleet Street near Deansgate, through a passage and into the garret of the house where Ann Ryan lived. The packages contained corsets that they had stolen from a draper's shop and when Caminada questioned the women, Ryan flew at him, pinioning him around the body and arms so that he could not move. The other two women opened the window and threw out the corsets, before fleeing down the stairs and out into the street. Still in Ryan's tight grip, Caminada dragged her down to the back yard, where he recovered the stolen goods. The inveterate felon was sentenced to a further two months.

Ann Ryan, who used a number of aliases, was convicted a record 19 times in 16 years, serving a total of almost three years in prison. Her convictions were invariably for begging and drunkenness and as Caminada concluded, Ann 'was a fair specimen of the average street beggar'.

Familiar with the ways of criminal women, Detective Caminada once used their technique of acting as bait to his own advantage, in order to apprehend a fraudulent businessman. When a senior partner of a firm in Manchester absconded, it was discovered that he was guilty of commercial fraud amounting to the enormous sum of £370,000. His creditors applied to the police for a warrant for his arrest, which was duly granted and entrusted to Detective Caminada. When he gained information from a reliable source that the culprit was living in Ilkley, a genteel town on the outskirts of Bradford, the detective travelled to West Yorkshire to investigate.

The purported residence of the errant businessman was a semi-detached villa with front and back gardens in a fashionable quarter of the town. The house was so quiet that Caminada had to resort to 'special use of ordinary means of influence' to identify the occupants. Knowing that young women enjoyed music, he hired a quartet band comprising a guitar, flute, harp and cornet to lure the serving girls into the garden, so that he could befriend them. When the band played a 'rollicking waltz' a maid appeared at one of the windows, but fearful of strangers, she ran back into the house. After the failure of his first attempt Caminada asked the guitarist to sing a plaintive tune about home. This time the ruse was successful and the back door of the villa opened to reveal two maids, who came out to listen to the music. The detective made a 'date' with the two maids for their day-off the following Sunday.

Despite his considerable effort, which included a walk in the woods, Caminada concluded that the owner of the villa was a retired banker from Dewsbury, who knew nothing of the fugitive. The next clue led Caminada to a small village near Otley, five miles from Bradford, where the businessman was believed to have been staying with a merchant friend. He travelled to the village with a former employee of the debtor and a young boy. The merchant's house was on the high road to Bradford and opened out on to a field. Whilst gathering information from the local gossips, Caminada met a butcher who regularly delivered supplies to the property. He offered the detective lodgings with his sister, from which Caminada had an excellent view of his target and was able to observe the merchant going about his daily business to and from the warehouse.

One evening there was a party in the garden of the house and, seeking an opportunity to gain entry, Caminada instructed the boy to kick a ball over the wall and then to knock at the door to retrieve it. The lad undertook the task, but it was still not possible to identify the absconded man, so Caminada decided it was time for another 'romantic episode' with one of the servants. When a couple of serving girls left the house to deposit some refuse, Caminada followed them, taking the boy with him so as not to arouse suspicion. Despite the initial reluctance of the young women to speak to him, the detective persevered: 'But I was not to be thrown off thus. I knew sufficiently the inquisitiveness and contrariness of lovely women'.

Discovering their plan to visit the wakes, a festival in a nearby village, he arranged to attend the fair with them. The following Saturday, amongst the roundabouts, side stalls and strolling musicians, Caminada solicited vital information as to the whereabouts of his missing man. One of the maids was originally from Prestwich in Manchester, where she had been in the employ of the suspect, but she had been warned not to mention him to anyone. Keen to find out more, Caminada invited her to Leeds on a pleasure trip. They hired a rowing boat on the lake in Roundhey Park and the detective, who was masquerading as an engineer, bought her a handsome umbrella as a gift.

His lavish attentions eventually paid off and after a short correspondence and another weekend in Harrogate, where they stayed in a hotel and enjoyed a dinner together, Caminada finally obtained the businessman's address. He fled straight back to Manchester and gave the details to the creditors. The case resolved, that left the delicate issue of disappointing the young maid: 'She was informed that her lover had become suddenly indisposed, and the news soon followed that he had departed to the land "where the wicked cease from troubling and the weary are at rest". Very much alive and still at the height of his career, Detective Chief Inspector Caminada was awarded an increase in his salary of 10 shillings per week by the watch committee on 18 June 1891 for 'meritorious conduct'.

Despite 'romancing' women in a professional capacity, by 1891 Jerome Caminada had been married for 10 years. After the tragic early years of his marriage, life had improved for the couple. His son, Charles Bernard was now a healthy three-year-old and on New Year's Eve 1890 his wife Amelia had given birth to their final child, a daughter, whom they named Mary. Both children, unlike their older siblings, would live long and healthy lives. During this time, the Caminadas had moved from Old Trafford to Chorlton-on-Medlock, not far from Amelia's family. Originally a small rural village, by the early 1890s it had been incorporated into Manchester's sprawling suburbs. The inner quarters were dominated by the Chorlton Mills complex and the sodden hovels of Little Ireland but further out, where the Caminada family lived, the area had remained gentrified with refined streets and spacious houses, which were home to prominent public figures such as the Gaskells and the Pankhursts. Caminada would live in this quarter for the rest of his life.

The other members of his family had not been so successful. His mother, aged 72, was an inmate of Barton-upon-Irwell Workhouse on the other side of the city. A retired tassel-maker, she had been blind for eight years and lived away from her family in the workhouse, where she was probably being cared for in the infirmary. She remained there until her death in 1895. It seems shocking that Caminada's mother ended her days in this way and it is impossible to understand why she was admitted to the workhouse in the first place. Unfortunately, no records of her time there have survived, so the full details of her circumstances remain unknown.

Mary Caminada's sad, difficult life in Manchester was the harsh reality for many women in the Victorian era. Towards the end of his career Caminada recalled visiting the City Gaol in 1870, when he was shocked to see the plight of female convicts as they were being unloaded from the prison van:

> *Out of the twenty-seven women and a child that alighted, there was not one that had a whole garment or a clean article about her, and misery of the deepest kind was to be seen in their pinched faces.*

Resorting to crime, many impoverished young girls joined gangs of scuttlers, or street fighters, which were a menace to society and a real challenge for police officers. However, Detective Caminada would go to considerable lengths to save the life of one scuttler.

Chapter Thirteen

Scuttlers and the Art of Gang Warfare (1892)

Many a good tussle have I had with other classes of criminals, but I would rather face the worst of these than a scuttler.
(Jerome Caminada *Twenty-Five Years of Detective Life*, 1901)

During the final three decades of the nineteenth century, gangs of 'scuttlers' or street fighters plagued the city of Manchester. As Detective Caminada experienced for the first time when still a young police officer, these groups of violent and ruthless youths would 'stand at nothing when their blood is up'. They were well-organised, fearless and, above all, highly dangerous. The usual deterrents of fines and prison sentences did not work on the scuttlers and the authorities were at a loss for effective methods to deal with them.

Scuttler gangs were territorial, taking their names from the streets where they lived. Andrew Davies in *The Gangs of Manchester*, gives examples including the Ordsall Lane and Hope Street gangs from Ordsall, Salford; the Clock Alley gang, which was named after an alleyway near Shudehill in the city centre; and the fearsome Bengal Tigers from Bengal Street in Ancoats. There were many others and each gang had their own 'patch', which they would defend to the death. Rival groups entered at their peril.

Journalist Alexander Devine wrote in the *Manchester Guardian* in 1890 that 'scuttlers' were young men (and often women too) between the ages of 14 and 19. Employed in factories, mills and foundries, they joined a gang after leaving school. The youths were highly style-conscious with a distinctive appearance; the boys dressed in flared trousers, known locally as 'narrow-go-wides', scarves and cloth caps. On their feet they wore narrow-toed, brass-tipped clogs, which doubled as vicious weapons, capable of inflicting bruises and fractures on their enemies. Their 'uniform' not only gave them status, but also acted as an invitation to incite rival gangs to try their luck against them.

Scuttlers were armed to the teeth with pokers, cutlasses, leather straps studded with iron bolts, bricks, bottles and knives – anything that could inflict harm on their enemies. The weapons of choice were stones (they would even use the cobbles from the streets) and belts. Their belt was the scuttlers' most treasured possession and their deadliest weapon. Made of leather, the belts were one to two inches wide and two or three feet long, with a large brass buckle at the end. In battle the fighters would swing the buckle around, inflicting cuts and lacerations to the head and face of an opponent. Often they drove nails through the end of the belt to make it even more lethal: a scuttler's belt could fracture skulls. The more important members and leaders of the gangs decorated their belts with brass pins in distinctive patterns and shapes, to reflect their lofty position in the hierarchy.

'Scuttles' took place throughout the city, on crofts, rough ground and even in the streets of busy neighbourhoods. A feud would spark between rival gangs and the resulting 'war' could continue for months with attacks and counterattacks, the violence spreading out into the local community. Terrified shopkeepers and café owners closed their businesses as soon as fights broke out. Passersby and shoppers scurried to safety. Sometimes two key members of rival gangs would engage in hand-to-hand combat and on other occasions, large-scale fights were organised, involving hundreds of youths. The timing and location of such battles were chalked on pavements in advance. Gangs would also invade the territory of others, inciting violent backlashes and calls for revenge. Girls were by no means excluded from the action and they would egg on their male companions, by handing them weapons and inciting them to fight harder.

As the objective of 'scuttling' was to maim and disfigure, there were very few deaths linked to the fighting. However, for some 30 years the local papers printed graphic accounts of gang warfare, and the hard-faced street fighters of Victorian Manchester posed a significant threat to the inhabitants of the city and not least of all to the police, as Detective Caminada discovered to his cost, in his early days as a constable.

During his first year on the beat there was an ongoing feud between the Clock Alley lads, from the back streets around Manchester Cathedral, and a gang from Greengate, just over the River Irwell in Salford. One night the Clock Alley gang entered enemy territory, but after a fierce battle they were defeated and repelled. The victors chased their foes over Victoria Bridge and back onto their own turf, where the battle recommenced. Constable Caminada happened to be passing at the time and, as he recalled later, 'having, perhaps, too exalted an opinion of the powers of a police officer and the majesty of the law', he pitched straight into the mêlée.

Despite his uniform Caminada had no impact whatsoever on the frenzied fighting and was rewarded for his attempt at bravery with bruises from cobblestones that the scuttlers pulled up from the street. Before long Caminada was laid out flat by a large stone, which hit him on the spine. Fortunately, when he went down the youths fled and he hobbled to the Dog and Partridge Public House nearby to recover from his wounds. The young police officer had learnt a valuable lesson.

A short while later, however, Caminada succeeded in exacting a small revenge. In a local neighbourhood he was struck on the back of the head by a missile thrown by a member of a gang. By this time he had acquired a thick ash walking stick with a heavy knot at one end and rushed into the group, striking them with it on all sides. His violent foray claimed two or three victims who fell dazed to the ground and before they had a chance to retaliate, he jumped onto a passing tramcar and made his escape.

Nevertheless, almost 25 years later, after many experiences of dealing with gang warfare, Caminada would undergo a major change of heart and find himself campaigning for the reprieve of a young scuttler convicted of murder. In the summer of 1890, gang fights and violence intensified on the streets of Manchester, with a series of long-running feuds all over the city. This 'epidemic' initiated heated debates on the subject amongst the authorities and in the press. On 12 December a deputation from the justices of Manchester and Salford went to London to meet with the Home Secretary, Henry Matthews, to request that power be granted to magistrates to sentence scuttlers to corporal punishment, specifically flogging. They recounted the terror being wrought on the community: 'the whole neighbourhood is in a state of great alarm, great damage being done to property and persons'.

The only recourse to justice then within their power was to levy fines on the culprits, ranging from 40 shillings to £20, or to give out short prison sentences of up to six months. In practice gangs simply rallied round to pay any fines incurred by their members and if a scuttler went to prison, he was hailed as a hero and promoted to a higher rank within the gang on his release. In the light of their experience, the delegates advocated an extension to the use of flogging, which was then used solely for juvenile offenders (under the age of 14) and for adult male serving prisoners, in cases of insubordination.

During the second half of the nineteenth century only higher courts could mete out corporal punishment for adults, and just for specific crimes such as robbery with violence. They had to stipulate whether the birch or the cat-o'-nine-tails was to be used and how many strokes were to be inflicted. Flogging would usually be combined with a custodial sentence, and in practice it was rare. However, for young offenders corporal punishment was much more common and those under 14 were often sentenced to birching or flogging, as well as short prison sentences.

Although Detective Caminada did not join the official debate, he advocated the use of physical punishment for young street fighters instead of custodial sentences, after witnessing at first-hand how incarceration was failing to work as a deterrent for offenders of all ages. In his memoirs he recollected standing by a spiral staircase in Strangeways Prison, watching prisoners return to the cells after their daily exercise. Five lads ranging from 12 to 14 years walked by in single file, supervised by a warder and they made faces at the police officer as they passed him. Caminada's instant reaction was to laugh at their antics, but he reflected later that:

> *The prison evidently had no terrors for them – a birch rod would have been far more effective. Prison discipline and its associations were evidently going to make them pests to society.*

This would have been a fairly standard view amongst nineteenth century law enforcers and in Caminada's opinion it would have been better to spare youngsters the corruptive influence of prison.

In the case of the scuttlers, they were mostly exempt from corporal punishment because they were usually older than the legal age of 14 and therefore were not classed as 'juvenile offenders'. The deputation from Manchester and Salford argued that the use of flogging had been so successful in eradicating garrotters, that it would also be an effective discouragement for street fighters. But the Home Secretary was reluctant to endorse their views. He explained that the House of Commons and the general public were increasingly averse to the use of corporal punishment, especially for older boys and men. He also expressed the difficulty in distinguishing between 'scuttlers' and other individuals engaged in riots, brawls and fist fights, and was quoted in the *Manchester Courier*:

> *There were multitudes in Trafalgar-square armed with gaspipes, sticks and stones. Your definition of scuttling would include this. Just imagine whether public feeling would allow the rioters of Trafalgar-square to be flogged.*

Instead, the Home Secretary proposed raising the legal age of juvenile offenders to 16 and the debate raged for the rest of the century, as the criminal justice system continued to evolve. In Manchester, scuttling showed no signs of abating and the violence would reach new heights with the death of one teenager at the hands of another.

On Thursday 21 April 1892, Billy Willan and his mates were returning home from work when they crossed the path of another group of youths. Willan, 16, was a cooper (barrel-maker), probably working with his uncle and cousins, who were wood turners. His three companions, also aged 16, were James Hand, a dyer's labourer, Edward Fleming and Charles Davidson. All four formed part of the Bradford Street gang in Ancoats. The other lads were in a rival gang from Lime Street, headed by Peter Kennedy, 16, who worked at Crabtree's dyeworks. The two gangs had been involved in an ongoing feud over girls.

According to the *Manchester Courier*, when Willan challenged Kennedy to a decisive scuttle to end the argument, he was humiliated by his opponent's flippant response and vowed revenge. Two days later about 1pm, after declaring he was going to 'dose' (stab) Kennedy, Willan gathered his supporters and, armed with a pocketknife, lay in wait for his rival. Davidson had a belt and Flemming, a stick. The two groups clashed and a fight broke out, resulting in Kennedy being stabbed in the back.

Although the events surrounding the attack were unclear, all fingers pointed to Billy Willan as the perpetrator. James Hand, who had left the scene before the incident, said that he had seen Willan later with the open knife, its blade bloodied. Allegedly he had boasted of using it on Kennedy. Peter Kennedy suffered a two-inch knife wound between his ribs and was transported to the Royal Infirmary. He lingered between life and death until 8 May, when he died of internal bleeding despite the best efforts of the surgeons to save him. What had started as a street brawl had ended in murder.

Billy Willan was arrested at his home and stood trial for the murder of Peter Kennedy on 20 May at the Manchester Assizes with his two companions. In court his friends testified against him, confirming that Billy was the one who struck the fatal blow with the knife. At the summing up, the Counsel for the Defence, Charles McKeand, appealed to the jury on Willan's behalf stating that he was: 'on the threshold of life, standing on the very brink of the awful abyss of death'. The young prisoners sobbed in the dock, as McKeand solemnly reminded the jurors that it was their duty to decide if the 'three little fellows' should live or die.

It took the jury just over an hour to reach their verdict: Willan was found guilty of wilful murder, with a strong recommendation for clemency due to his youth. Flemming and Davidson were acquitted. Following this grim pronouncement the judge donned the black cap and passed the death sentence. Terror-stricken, Willan cried out, 'Oh, master, don't: I'm only 16'. The *Manchester Courier* described the traumatic scene:

> *He became so frantic that two policemen in the dock had to seize him and hold him by the arms until the sentence was completed. He was then removed. Several females in the gallery, among whom we believe was the mother of the prisoner, betrayed great agitation, screaming and uttering wild cries.*

As Willan was led away to Strangeways Prison, the campaign to save him from the gallows began in earnest. His solicitor initiated a petition for presentation to the Home Secretary, requesting a commutation of the death sentence to penal servitude for life. It outlined the case and stated that Willan had been of good character until he became involved with a gang of scuttlers. Although Caminada had not been involved directly in this case, he received a note from the governor of Strangeways, informing him that the condemned lad had asked to see him.

Always ready to respond to a plea for help, he visited Willan in gaol. Even though he had been visiting the prison for some 20 years, this was the first time the detective had ever stepped into a condemned cell and the experience shook him to the core. The scene that unfolded would remain with him for the rest of his life:

> *The poor lad put his arms through the bars which separated us, and, with tears streaming down his cheeks, implored me to save him. I was much affected, and promised that I would do all in my power towards this end.*

As he was leaving the prison Caminada met a woman with a shawl over her head, who seized him by the hand. She was Hannah Willan, Billy's mother and she begged Caminada to spare her son. After these emotional encounters, Caminada joined the campaign for Willan's reprieve, and soon after, on 30 May 1892, the governor of Strangeways announced that Billy Willan's death sentence had been commuted to one of penal servitude for life. Caminada had fulfilled the promise made to the lad and his mother, but he was unaware that there would be an unexpected and astonishing dénouement to the case.

Following his narrow escape from the scaffold, Billy Willan served eight years in Strangeways for the murder of Peter Kennedy. He was released in 1900 and returned to his work as a cooper, living alone in Harpurhey, on the edge of the city. Five years later, on 22 March 1905, he married Florence

Caminada at Prestwich Register Office. Florence, 27, was the daughter of Jerome's brother, John Baptiste. The couple remained in Manchester and their son, George William Louis, was born the following year on 15 June, just over 14 years after Willan had received the death sentence. In 1911 the family was living in Collyhurst, where Billy ran a fish and chip shop, not far from the scene of the incident that could easily have ended his life.

Billy Willan went on to lead an ordinary and respectable life until his death in 1951, at the age of 75. However, not all criminals could be reformed and Caminada encountered many heartless men who exploited their relationships with women for their own gain and who, despite efforts to change them, would never make good husbands.

Chapter Fourteen

False Lovers and Wily Seducers
(1892–1893)

It is a case, Watson, which may prove to have something in it, or may prove to have nothing, but which, at least, presents those unusual and outré features which are as dear to you as they are to me.

(Sir Arthur Conan Doyle,
The Adventure of the Stock-Broker's Clerk, 1893)

Like Sherlock Holmes, Detective Caminada loved nothing more than a puzzling case to test his skills of detection. Therefore, when he received a report of a suspected overdose from the Assistant-Commissioner of the CID in London, he soon realised there was more to this incident than met the eye.

At 8.15pm on 18 August 1892, the police were called to an address in Marylebone. When the landlord let them in, they discovered a middle-aged woman lying in an unconscious state. There was an unlabelled bottle of chloroform on a chair beside the bed. The doctor in attendance poured a large glass of brandy down her throat before the police took her to the 'insane ward' of the nearest infirmary, where she was revived. When she came to, the woman gave her name as Lucilla Roberts. Originally from Kendal, she lived in Manchester and said that her husband was currently staying on the Isle of Man.

The following day Mrs Roberts was well enough for a formal interview and she made a full statement to the local police. Aged 50, she had married her legal adviser six months earlier, but had not seen him since the wedding. A distant relative of hers, James Eckersley Thompson, had kept her informed of her husband's whereabouts, acting as messenger between the newly-weds until they could be reunited. When she last met Thompson at Cadishead, on the outskirts of Manchester, two days before, he had given her some medicine for a skin rash from Mr Roberts and instructed her to travel to London, where her husband would join her later. Mrs Roberts took lodgings in Marylebone and the following morning after breakfast, she poured out the contents of the bottle into a glass and drank it. She remembered nothing more until she woke up in the hospital. At the end of her statement she avowed that she did not believe that either Thompson or her husband had wished her any harm in directing her to take the draught.

When Mrs Roberts mentioned her circumstances, the police became increasingly suspicious. She did not know where her husband was and, after having recently sold two houses with James Thompson taking care of the profits, she was now penniless. As her former properties were in Manchester, the CID contacted Detective Inspector Caminada. The detective's first port of call was Mrs Roberts's solicitor in Manchester, who confirmed that he had acted on her behalf in the sale of her house in Whalley Range. The property had sold for £450, an appropriate price for a large house at the time, and Thompson, to whom she referred as her nephew, had been present as her companion throughout the proceedings. After the transaction Thompson had taken the money for Mrs Roberts, explaining that this was just in case she mislaid it and promising to pass it on to her husband, as he had done with previous sales. He had also apparently purchased at least one of her houses for himself.

As the investigation progressed, Caminada realised that he had already made the acquaintance of the woman, who was also known as Miss Prescott. She regularly made complaints at the town hall about disturbances in her neighbourhood. The detective knew James Thompson too, a local baker's son, and had recently seen him pawning some spoons, so he knew that he did not have the means to buy houses. 'There was certainly a mystery attached to the case, and this mystery it was my duty to clear up', Caminada concluded.

His next step was to track down the enigmatic Thomas Roberts, husband of Lucilla Prescott. The detective paid a visit to another firm of solicitors mentioned in the police report and this revealed the first in a series of startling twists in the tale. Mr Roberts was indeed a solicitor, but he had been married for more than 20 years and had a family. He indignantly denied all suggestions that he was romantically linked with Miss Prescott, stating that she was merely a former client who had made a complaint against one of the clerks of the firm, a tenant of hers who had refused to pay his rent. He concluded that the accusation was an absolute lie from beginning to end and that 'they had always considered her to be more or less out of her mind, particularly on the question of marriage'. He knew nothing of any attempt to poison her and had not seen her since 1888.

It was now obvious that Lucilla's young relative, James Thompson was the key to solving the mystery, and so, through Thompson's solicitor, Caminada arranged to meet Thompson at his house in Cadishead. In reply to the detective's questions, Thompson admitted that he had bought Miss Prescott's house and some furniture for £500. At the mention of the pawned spoons, he confessed that he had stolen the money from his father's till. He denied knowing anyone with the name of Roberts. Ignoring his protestations of innocence, on 16 September Caminada and his officers arrested Thompson on suspicion of theft, fraud and having administered poison to Miss Lucilla Prescott with intent to murder her. The detective accompanied Miss Prescott to Thompson's house, where she identified her furniture. A letter found at the property to Thompson from his wife, from whom he had been estranged, revealed that he had also assumed the role of Roberts.

Despite this sophisticated and convincing plot, Caminada was still perplexed by the question of how Miss Prescott could have fallen for Thompson's charms to such an extent that she had lost all her properties and worldly goods. He was shocked to discover that a bizarre flaw in her character had led to her downfall: 'there was unravelled the most remarkable evidence, which read more like fiction than fact'. In spite of being an otherwise intelligent and able businesswoman, Lucilla Prescott was under the delusion that every man she met would fall in love with her, and wished to marry her without delay. The son of a close friend of hers, James Thompson had cleverly exploited her weakness.

When Thompson's mother had died in 1886, she had asked Lucilla to take care of James. As he grew up James visited Miss Prescott's house frequently and they became friends, with Lucilla confiding her secrets in this seemingly pleasant young man. When Thompson's father supposedly withdrew his income, James turned to his older friend for support. In the winter of 1891, he moved into Miss Prescott's house and his 'nefarious designs' began.

In his attempt to steal her money, Thompson created imaginary scenarios to gain her trust. He pretended that a gentleman who admired her greatly, had asked Thompson to support him in his quest to marry her. This fictitious suitor was the mysterious Mr Roberts. Thompson convinced Miss Prescott to say that she was already married to Roberts so that her lover could rid himself of a jealous ex-lover, an Italian dancer at the Palace of Varieties, with a fierce Mediterranean temper. She even bought herself a wedding ring on her husband's behalf to complete the fiction. During the next few months Lucilla received instructions from 'Thomas Roberts' to travel all over the British Isles, which she did in the hope of meeting him at last. Her final destination was London, where she was urged to drink the potentially fatal bottle of chloroform that would put an end to this diabolical charade.

The trial of James Thompson took place on 27 September 1892. In a full courtroom he was convicted of fraud and sentenced to 12 months' imprisonment. There had been no proof of his attempt to poison Lucilla Prescott, so for that crime he went unpunished. His deluded victim had learnt her lesson and she remained single until her death in 1903.

Sham marriages were not unusual in Victorian England. Before the Matrimonial Causes Act of 1857, divorce was only possible through a private act of Parliament. Even after the Act, it was virtually impossible for ordinary people, and particularly for women, to end their marriage legally, due to prohibitive costs and the complicated nature of the procedure. Consequently, some unhappy spouses chose simply to leave and move to a different part of the country as a final resort. However, if these absentee spouses wished to marry again, they would do so as a bigamist. Detective Caminada encountered one such case that astounded the people of Manchester.

Leonard Ratcliffe, aged 38, was well-known in musical circles in the city. A clerk at the Diocesan Registry, he married Katherine Parr in St Ann's Church on the fashionable square of the same name, where he was choirmaster. He was also a chorister at Manchester Cathedral and seemingly respectable. When Katherine had met her future husband four years earlier, he had told her that he was a widower. In reality, Leonard was leading a double life, which included previous convictions for fraud and, worse still, an abandoned wife and children.

A tall and distinguished-looking man, Leonard Ratcliffe was familiar to the regular worshippers of the cathedral, who were shocked when his shady past came to light. Ratcliffe's first marriage had taken place in 1881, to Mary Kate Dutson. The couple married in Handsworth near Birmingham, where they set up home. Ratcliffe's first disappearance was in 1885, when he fled to Ireland following some trouble with forged bills. He returned to his wife, but left once again when it was discovered that he had been falsifying the books of his business. This happened several times more, with Leonard's departures always following suspicions of financial double-dealing.

He finally absconded for good in 1890, leaving his wife with their five children, including triplets; she did not hear from him again. His second wife only learned of his bigamy when Caminada produced Ratcliffe's two marriage certificates at his arrest, by which time she was expecting their first child. At the trial Ratcliffe had no defence to offer for his actions and was sentenced to three years' penal servitude. Both Leonard Ratcliffe's 'wives' were forced to manage on their own because of his deceit, but for some women, everyday life with their husband meant habitual violence and domestic abuse.

When Detective Caminada met a woman being attacked in the street, he wasted no time in sorting out her assailant. He was on duty one morning in Charter Street, one of the roughest parts of the city, when a woman ran screaming past him, with a large man in pursuit. Before Caminada's eyes, the man overtook the woman and struck her two violent blows, knocking her to the ground. He then started to kick her about the body like a football as she shrieked in terror. Without a moment's hesitation Caminada ran to her rescue: 'Losing all command of myself I rushed at the fiend'. He struck the man in the face with his fist, using such force that he dropped to the pavement where his head smashed against the cobbles, knocking him unconscious.

By this time a crowd had gathered and another officer came to help. They pulled the man to his feet and, as they walked him in the direction of the police station, he seized his captors so hard that he tore a large patch out of the other officer's uniform trousers, ripping them from top to bottom. Caminada subdued him again with more punches; one so hard that the detective thought he had broken his own arm. As Caminada was leaving the police station to have his arm checked at the infirmary, the man made a final bid for freedom and rushed out into the yard. Not realising that the outer gate was closed he hurtled into it, dashing his head against the wood. The next morning the prisoner appeared before the magistrates and, as the police could not induce his wife to testify against him, he received just two months' imprisonment.

Caminada's arm was only strained, but he suffered with it for months afterwards, unable even to turn a door handle without pain. However, his efforts had not been in vain: 'I had the satisfaction of knowing that I had administered to the big bully a thrashing he was not likely soon to forget'.

During the Victorian era the law was slowly altered to afford women more protection. Until 1841 rape had been a capital offence, but this had had the deleterious effect of reducing the number of rape charges, as juries were not keen to commit an offender to the gallows. Following the removal of the crime from the list of capital offences reports of rape increased, reaching a hiatus in 1846. Throughout the rest of the century trials for sexual crimes continued to rise, especially after the raising of the age of consent from 12 to 13 in 1875. (It was raised once more, to 16, in 1885).

Despite these developments rape and other sexual offences were still notoriously difficult to prove and were often treated as 'assault', carrying more lenient sentences than theft or larceny. In 1893 Detective Caminada investigated a very serious case of indecent assault. An advertisement appeared in a London newspaper, offering young ladies the chance to work in a new Parisian women's clothing show-room opening in Manchester. A generous salary of £60 was offered, as well as board and lodgings. Applicants were invited to send a full-length photograph showing their style of figure, to Alphonse Redfern of 'Robes, Modes, Lingerie and Corsets'. They also had to state their age and were required to dress well in gowns and underwear, as the company, which sold high quality women's clothing, was very particular about its staff.

Tempted by this offer, many young women submitted applications and soon received a reply informing them of their success at the initial stage. The next step in the process was the purchase of a tailor-made French gown in black satin with a train, from the company. They could buy the dress at a discounted cost of 4 guineas, rather than the usual 10, and it would, the letter stated, improve their figure on the shop floor. After some further correspondence, the successful applicants were invited to travel to Manchester, at their own expense, to view the new premises and meet the proprietor, Alphonse Redfern.

Young ladies flocked to the store and Redfern, who said he was the nephew of the well-known firm of Redfern Ltd Paris, took three of them to a boarding house in Salford. He engaged one to write letters to subsequent applicants, another to find a suitable residence for the female assistants, and the third to send for catalogues and samples for furnishing. He also accompanied them to the new premises at Grosvenor Chambers, Deansgate, which they viewed from the outside.

A few days after their arrival, Redfern was walking down the road with one of the young women, when they passed a photographer's studio with pictures of actors and actresses in the window. They stopped to look and he told her that she would be required to model fancy dress costumes, some of which would be above the knee. Later that evening after supper, he said that he was required to take her measurements himself, as his manageress was unavailable. Reassuring her that in Paris, men always took women's measurements, he instructed her to remove her dress and measured her around the ankle, calf and above the knee. When he asked her to take off her underwear she refused and he stopped. Before leaving he requested her to send one of the other women to him.

When the second young woman, a 20-year-old from Norwood, South London, arrived he repeated the procedure, saying that he found it an unpleasant task but he was obliged to do it because of the continuing absence of his manageress. After initially refusing, she agreed to remove her dress so that he could measure her chest and, that done, she then put out her foot for the final measurement. Redfern knelt on the floor, took hold of her ankle and committed an indecent assault. The terrified woman ran screaming from the room and one of the other assistants accompanied her to the detective office.

Caminada returned to the firm's offices with the women to question Alphonse Redfern. When asked for references to prove his identity, Redfern could not produce any, so the detective took him into custody. Finding only £5 on his person, he questioned the suspect about the money the women had given him for the dresses. Redfern offered to reimburse the money in exchange for his release, but Caminada charged him with obtaining money by false pretences, indecent assault and procuring women for immoral purposes, to which the prisoner replied, 'I am not so bad as you think I am'.

Alphonse Redfern had no connection with the company of the same name in Paris and they stated that it was not their practice to measure shop assistants in their underwear. The case aroused great public interest and on 16 June 1893, Alphonse Redfern was found guilty and sentenced to 12 months for obtaining money under false pretences and six for indecent assault, the sentences to be served concurrently. The judge concluded that: 'the prisoner had committed a cruel fraud on these young people, an abominable sort of crime'. On his release Redfern was re-arrested for similar offences in London.

When he recalled the case later, Detective Caminada gave a grave warning to other potential victims:

There are few frauds of a worse kind than those by which respectable girls are induced to leave their homes. Finding themselves destitute amongst strangers they become an easy prey to the wily seducer.

Since 1828, the law had considered sexual relations with a child under 10 a 'felony' and with a child between 10 and 12, a 'misdemeanour'. The crime of indecent assault included 'attempted carnal knowledge' with anyone under the age of 12. Detective Caminada uncovered a scandalous crime of this nature, committed by a prominent and upstanding member of society.

A young boy was on an errand from the warehouse where he worked, when he met a man near the Manchester Royal Infirmary. The older man engaged him in conversation and asked him to accompany him down one of the adjoining back streets, but the boy refused because he was keen to return to work. The man followed the child back to the factory, where he asked for his name. Some days later the boy received a message through the post saying,

Dear John, meet me tonight at 7.30 at the corner of Ardwick Green, opposite Rusholme-road. You will remember that I met you ten or twelve days ago in Mosley-street. You can bring your friend with you.

The boy took the letter straight to Caminada, who instructed him to meet the man at the appointed time. At a quarter past seven, the boy was standing ready at the meeting place when, 15 minutes later, the man arrived. He led the boy through several streets to a dark passage, where he presented him with a gold pencil case. A short while later Caminada appeared from the shadows and caught the man in the act of indecently exposing himself. As he arrested him, the man tried to bribe the detective with the offer of a sovereign and when his first attempt failed, he attacked Caminada with a thick walking stick. Caminada defended himself against his tall and powerful assailant as well as he could until assistance arrived, breaking his police staff in the fight. The prisoner was finally overpowered by five men and taken to the police station.

It transpired that the perpetrator of this shocking crime was a magistrate from Cheshire. He admitted the assault on Caminada, but denied all charges of indecency. On the other side of the bench for a change, he was found guilty and fined £20 for assaulting a police officer, £5 for the assault of a witness and just £2 for indecent exposure. Clearly the magistrate had considered himself to be above the law.

Chapter Fifteen

The Anarchists of Ardwick Green
(September 1893)

In the wake of the Industrial Revolution the people of Manchester played a radical role in the politics of protest. Home to trade unionism, the Anti-Corn Law League and Chartism, the city experienced demonstrations, campaigns and rioting throughout the nineteenth century. Detective Caminada was called upon many times to protect the general public, especially when the anarchists took to the streets in the 1890s.

In 1892 Caminada masterminded a successful operation to maintain order at the annual May Day demonstrations. The procession, comprising some 20,000 participants, banners and brass bands ended in Alexandra Park, where it was estimated that as many as 100,000 people gathered to hear speakers from political organisations and societies. Common themes for discussion were the eight-hour working day, adult suffrage and the formation of an independent labour party. Caminada and his 300 officers kept the peace and, according to the *Manchester Weekly Times*: 'The utmost order and decorum were maintained'.

However, operations did not always run so smoothly for the detective and he often had to defend himself against physical attacks, as well as slurs on his reputation. The following year he became embroiled in a bitter struggle with a local anarchist group, who vehemently defended their right to freedom of speech and resisted all Caminada's attempts to disperse them.

In September 1893 the Reverend Canon Nunn, rector of St Thomas's Church on the edge of Ardwick Green, lodged a complaint about the Manchester Anarchist Group, which held open-air meetings every Sunday on the green. Their soapbox speeches caused an obstruction on the pavements and subjected his flock to strong language, as they made their way home after the service. Chief Constable Malcolm Wood negotiated with the demonstrators, suggesting that they use Stevenson Square, a popular meeting place for speakers close to the city centre, or one of the police drill yards instead of Ardwick Green, which was a public park. The anarchists refused and persisted in meeting at their chosen spot.

A month later Detective Caminada accompanied the chief constable to the weekly gathering of the Manchester Anarchist Group. The first speaker was Charles Pellier, a Belgian, who mounted a chair to address the crowd of several hundred people. As his speech was of a 'revolutionary character', the chief constable asked Caminada to send Pellier a message that he wished to speak with him. Pellier agreed to step down, reluctant to get into trouble with the police because he had a wife and family. After advising his comrades to disperse, he walked away. The next person to take the chair was a young man named Alfred Barton. He was pulled down immediately by the police, only to be replaced by Patrick McCabe, a mechanic.

When McCabe was also dragged from his stand, there was a general rush of people at the handful of police officers in attendance. Barton grabbed the chair and struck a blow at Detective Caminada, hitting him violently in the chest, while someone else delivered a punch to Caminada's head, knocking off his hat. The unarmed detective struck out with his umbrella to defend himself. He was spared further injury but his umbrella broke in the fray. The police arrested four men, including Henry Burrows, a 19-year-old clerk, who was overheard remarking: 'If I had a revolver I would blow the damned policeman's brains out'.

The following day the prisoners appeared before the magistrate. The public gallery was full of friends and supporters of the defendants. In the dock beside Burrows, were Patrick McCabe aged 20; William Haughton, a pattern maker, also 20; and Ernest Stockton, an engineer aged 19. The hearing was interspersed with heckling, shouting and general chaos, as the defendants argued that they had been refused their right to freedom of speech. Haughton complained that they had been already tried and condemned in the press and Burrows accused the police of lying. The stipendiary, Mr Headlam, allowed the defendants' friends to testify, but eventually his patience ran out amid the derisive laughter and hissing, and he cleared the court.

Despite repeated orders for calm, the rest of the hearing was noisy and chaotic as the prisoners cross-examined the witnesses in a loud and insolent manner. Haughton remarked that Caminada, like all policemen, had a bad memory. He informed the bench that he weighed just 6 stone 5 pounds and posed no physical threat, to which Caminada retorted that Haughton weighed a good deal more in cheek. Despite further scenes of uproar, all the evidence was given and the defendants were fined 21 shillings and costs. The magistrate also ordered them to pay for the damage to Detective Caminada's umbrella. On hearing the verdict, one of the prisoners raised a cry of 'Hurrah for Anarchy!' and as Alfred Barton left the court, he shouted, 'To hell with law and order'. He was immediately re-arrested and Mr Headlam bound him over to keep the peace for six months.

The first ever prosecution of anarchists in Manchester was immortalised in a ballad about Caminada and his 'gamp' (umbrella). Sung to the tune of 'Monte Carlo', 'The Scamp who Broke his Gamp at Ardwick Green' recounts the events in seditious and irreverent detail:

> *And he walks about the street,*
> *With an independent air,*
> *The people all do swear,*
> *He is a detective rare,*
> *For he can lie,*
> *And none can vie-*
> *In the list of scamps, none stands so high*
> *As the D (detective) who broke his gamp at Ardwick Green, O.*
>
> *But the time is coming quickly when Cam will repent*
> *Of having tried his game*
> *The Anarchists to lame,*
> *Or he and his damned crew will to that warm land be sent,*
> *And never trouble honest folk again.*
>
> *And he walks along the court,*
> *With a hanging vicious air,*
> *The people will declare,*
> *Oh! What an awful scare.*
> *And they will cry,*
> *Oh! Let him die,*
> *And deep down in the gutter lie*
> *The D who broke his gamp at Ardwick Green, O.*

One of the regular anarchist speakers, taxidermist Patrick John Kelly, likened the umbrella incident to the unimaginable possibility of the government charging the Featherstone miners in Pontefract for the bullets with which they were shot during the strike earlier that year. He was arrested and fined for his comments. Undeterred, the anarchists continued to meet every Sunday morning on Ardwick Green to share their political views. Through the distribution of handbills, and perhaps also due to the recent publicity stirred by the court case, they encouraged more spectators and the meetings swelled in size, much to the displeasure of local residents.

During the next two months there was a succession of arrests and fines, as the defiant anarchists battled with police for dominance. Crowds of three to four thousand onlookers gathered each week and local tavern owners opened their bars, enjoying a roaring trade. People listened to speakers such as James Coates, a lithographic printer, who delivered a vitriolic speech denigrating Canon Nunn and Detective Caminada for interfering with the anarchists' right to express their views. The numbers of arrests increased exponentially.

On 5 November 21-year-old mechanic James Birch mounted the rostrum, waving a rolled up newspaper as a baton. His speech came to an abrupt end, when a number of youths let off fireworks into the crowd, accompanied by the cry, 'Duck him in the horse trough'. The police rescued Birch from his watery fate, and promptly arrested him. Two days later, when anarchist Santiago Salvador detonated two bombs in the Liceu Theatre, Barcelona, killing 22 people, the meetings in Manchester took a more serious turn. At the following meeting Herbert Stockton, another regular speaker and relative of the anarchist arrested during the umbrella incident, declared that they were determined to hold meetings, in spite of opponents such as Canon Nunn. After his arrest he was overheard discussing with a comrade that they should resort to extreme measures, as in Spain. Later in court Stockton said that he had been joking and refused to pay the customary fine, opting to go to prison instead. Others followed suit, choosing imprisonment over fines, and the deadlock held fast.

By the beginning of December, public interest was waning and the Sunday meetings were less well attended. In the wake of the Barcelona bombings financial support for the group had also dwindled. No one appeared on Christmas Eve, which Caminada commented was because 'none of them were inclined to eat their Christmas dinner in the police station'. On the last Sunday of 1893, the final meeting of the Manchester Anarchist Group took place on Ardwick Green; after a battle of three months the police and local residents were allowed to enjoy their Sundays in peace at last.

However, Detective Caminada soon became involved in another battle for free speech, which threatened not only his integrity as a police officer, but also his allegiance to his faith.

A meeting was planned by the Protestant Alliance at the YMCA Hall in central Manchester, during which ex-Roman Catholic priest Joseph Slattery would deliver a speech in opposition to 'Romish doctrines and practices'. As the date for the meeting approached, the secretary of the Catholic Truth Society published an article in the Roman Catholic newspaper *The Monitor and Catholic Standard and Ransomer,* suggesting that Slattery was known for intemperance, and his lectures had caused serious rioting in America.

A few days later, leaflets flooded the poorer quarters of the city and large posters announced the forthcoming lecture at the YMCA by Slattery and his wife, who was rumoured to be an escaped nun. This caused considerable consternation amongst the city's Catholics, especially in the Irish community. The police began to fear a major disturbance, which was exacerbated when another lecture given by an ex-Catholic priest at Central Hall led to some rowdy behaviour.

After repeated warnings in the press and private letters, the Lord Mayor sent for the Deputy Chief Constable, Walter Fell Smith, who instructed Caminada to prevent the meeting from going ahead. The detective was troubled by the order: 'This was a rather serious business for me, and I pointed out that, being a Catholic, I was likely to be accused of not acting impartially if I took any part in the matter'. He insisted on a special resolution from the watch committee or a written authority from the lord mayor, before he would take matters further.

On the day of the meeting, Caminada received the necessary papers and asked the stipendiary magistrate to clarify the extent of police powers to close public meetings. The judiciary confirmed that the police had no such power. Caminada reported back to Deputy Chief Constable Fell Smith, who subsequently positioned his men near the venue and ordered Caminada to advise the secretary of the YMCA to cancel the meeting. At 6pm, when people began turning up at the hall they found a notice on the door announcing that the meeting had been suspended. A great furore broke out and local people complained bitterly about the partiality of the police, on the grounds of religious discrimination. As an openly devout Catholic, Detective Caminada soon became the main target for their invective.

Shortly afterwards, the watch committee held an enquiry into the matter, during which the secretary of the YMCA denied that he had sought the interference of the police, and said that he had fully expected the meeting to take place. Deputy Chief Constable Fell Smith testified that Caminada had acted entirely without his knowledge. The committee concluded that the result had been a 'misunderstanding' between Chief Inspector Caminada and the secretary, Mr Newett. This unfortunate event gave rise to further anti-Catholic feeling and the police were accused of being under the control of Irish officers. Debates raged in the press and Caminada was accused of promoting his interests as a Catholic above his role as a police officer.

Throughout the uproar Detective Caminada defended his position, stating that he was simply doing his duty, in accordance with the deputy chief constable's orders. When Fell Smith issued a private circular arguing that the action had been taken without his knowledge, Caminada was outraged and commented later in his memoirs: 'Here, then, is a deliberate attempt of the Deputy chief constable to shift the blame off his own shoulders on to mine'. The city council later exonerated Caminada, but the detective was hurt by his superior's apparent betrayal. His relationship with Fell Smith never recovered and it would haunt him for the rest of his career.

Although the Slattery affair eventually died down, Detective Caminada was deeply agitated by the accusations levelled against him. A working class man of Irish extraction, this was one of the few occasions about which he was moved to share his own political views and feelings. Whilst he was not a supporter of anarchism, or even socialism, Caminada sympathised with those who advocated equality for all, as he was well aware of how difficult it was for a manual worker to survive on a weekly salary of 18 shillings, with high rents and food prices. In his view the real culprits were the owners of the mills and factories: 'Firms like these hold labour in their hands and squeeze out the heart's blood of the people'.

His real pet hate, however, were the 'middle-class do-gooders' and 'feather-brained zealots' who promoted societies for the greater good and 'moral progress' of others: 'One society is for putting out our pipes, another is for cutting off our beer, and a third regards beef as a source of evil'. In his memoirs he railed against the hypocrisy of the do-gooders' support for the right to free speech, at the same time as imposing limitations on the social life of ordinary working people, lest it divert them from their everyday task of manual labour. He wrote: 'if they could, they would have shut him (the working man) off from the free air of the country, and seal him up hermetically within the streets of his own grimy town'.

Despite his own elevation in society, Detective Caminada never forgot his origins and he remained adamant in his criticism of those who looked down, with thinly-disguised scorn, on the more unfortunate inhabitants of the city.

Chapter Sixteen

The Blackley Mystery and
other Suspicious Deaths
(November 1893)

D uring the Bank Holiday weekend in August 1893, three young brothers were playing in the woods at Dark Hole Clough, in Blackley, near Manchester. Whilst they were hunting for blackberries it began to rain and the boys took shelter under the trees. From their refuge Alfred Shorrocks, aged 12, spotted what he thought was a red flower. On closer inspection he found that it was a parcel wrapped in brown paper, partly hidden beneath some shrubs. When Alfred poked it with a stick the paper ripped to reveal a child's cap. He opened the parcel and, to his horror, discovered the body of a baby boy.

The lads raced to a nearby cottage and alerted the owner, William Henry Birch, who accompanied them back to the woods. After examining the infant to check that he was not breathing, Birch took the tiny corpse to a police mortuary, where police surgeon, Dr Rudovich Young, examined the body. The doctor estimated that the well-nourished child had been dead for four to six days. There were no signs of violence on the body and the cause of death was asphyxia, probably due to convulsions. The coroner later returned a verdict of death by natural causes and the unidentified infant was buried in Manchester General Cemetery in Harpurhey.

The case might have ended there had it not been for a hotel owner who contacted the police after reading about the incident in the local press. Mary Ann King was the landlady of the Central Temperance Hotel in New Bridge Street, near Victoria Railway Station. The report had reminded her of a young woman, who had been confined in her hotel in July. Giving her name as 'Mrs Allen' and claiming to be the wife of an army officer absent on duty, the heavily-pregnant woman had arrived two months prior to her child's birth. Mrs King had arranged for a doctor to attend Mrs Allen while she waited for her confinement.

The landlady added that Mrs Allen had met her 'uncle' every day at the station, right up until the birth of the child on 4 July. Afterwards she resumed the daily visits, leaving her son in the care of Mrs King. At the end of July Mrs Allen announced that she was moving back to her hometown of Kirkby Lonsdale, in Cumbria. After buying feeding bottles and brown paper, she left with the child the following day to catch the 11am train. Concerned, Mrs King followed the mother and child to the railway station, but when she arrived they had disappeared.

Detective Caminada accompanied Mrs King to the police station where, after she had identified the deceased child's clothing as that of Mrs Allen's baby, the investigation began. Around the same time, enquiries were initiated on behalf of Mrs Frances Remington, a cook, whose step-daughter had been missing since the previous May. Elizabeth Ann Remington, 25, had been in service away from home as a domestic servant and, despite being engaged to be married to a young man called Albert Barnesley, she had mysteriously disappeared whilst visiting her cousin in Morecambe. Her fiancé had written to the cousin, only to discover that Elizabeth Ann had never arrived in Morecambe. Every effort was made to trace her but without success, until Mrs Remington decided it was time to call the police.

As the investigation into the unknown child's death gathered pace, Elizabeth Ann Remington suddenly turned up to see her stepmother in Rochdale. When Mrs Remington suggested that Elizabeth had been having an illicit relationship with her employer, her step-daughter was outraged and denied all accusations. However, on 28 September Caminada and his colleague took the landlady, Mrs King, to Burnley, where she identified Elizabeth Ann Remington as 'Mrs Allen', the mother of the deceased infant. The detective arrested Elizabeth Ann on suspicion of having murdered her illegitimate child. Throughout the investigation it had been presumed that the father of the infant was a 'man of substance', as this would explain his motive for concealing the birth in order to preserve his reputation. In her statement to the police Elizabeth Ann confirmed that this was the case.

Ashworth Read, aged 47, was a cotton waste dealer, who owned Spruce Mill. Married with four children, the youngest of whom was four years old, he lived with his family in Burnley. According to the 1891 census they employed one domestic servant: Elizabeth Ann Remington. When Read discovered that Elizabeth was pregnant with his child, he moved her to Manchester, where they met every day at the station.

On the day of the child's death, Elizabeth Ann stated that they had taken the tram with the child to Cheetham Hill and entered the woods at Blackley.

She recalled that Read had soaked a handkerchief in water and given it to her to place on the child's mouth, which she did. After removing it, Read repeated the action and shortly after the child was dead. He wrapped the body in brown paper and left it unburied there in the woods, where the Shorrocks brothers found it. Perhaps Read had hoped that the body would be eaten by animals and become unidentifiable.

Detective Caminada went to the Royal Exchange, where Read was well known as a regular trader and arrested him. He charged them both with murder, but apart from Elizabeth Ann's testimony there was still no concrete evidence to link Read to the case, so Caminada began to piece together the events that had led to the gruesome discovery in the woods at Blackley.

The detective quickly confirmed the connection between the suspects, before and after the child was born. The son of the hotelkeeper, nine-year-old James King, identified the prisoners and said that he had seen them together several times, whilst he was playing in the street. Other witnesses came forward to corroborate his statement. A publican had noticed them taking tea together in his tavern and William Gordon, caretaker of St Michael's Flags, the site of a former paupers' graveyard near Angel Meadow, had seen both the prisoners regularly throughout May and June. Read would bring food and the pair would sit there together for a while. He had not noticed whether Elizabeth Ann was pregnant, but he saw her crying on two occasions. James Bartholomew, the verger of nearby St Michael and All Angels' Church, also spotted the couple on the Flags. He said that they usually stayed for about an hour and once, when she had dropped her mackintosh, he had thought that Elizabeth might be expecting a child.

Caminada also acquired the evidence of a tobacconist, John Waters, who said that the prisoners had entered his newsagent's on New Bridge Street, to take shelter from the rain. He remembered offering Elizabeth Ann a chair because she looked ill. The final witness statement was from John Stone, a detective at Victoria Railway Station. He had seen the couple in the station refreshment room and on platform six, from which the trains ran to Burnley. The case was building and, when Caminada discovered letters from Elizabeth's fiancé at Read's mill, he was certain that both suspects were guilty. In order to secure his conviction Caminada produced evidence from a tram guard who recognised the prisoners; they had travelled in his tramcar towards Cheetham Hill at 1pm on the day of the murder. The guard, Henry Spencer, confirmed that they had alighted at the tram office with the child. Another tram guard, Matthew Peam, saw the woman returning alone at about 2.30pm. He had noticed her because she kept bursting into tears.

At the end of October Ashworth Read and Elizabeth Ann Remington appeared at the Manchester Police Court and, after the initial hearing, the case was referred to the Assizes in Liverpool. Before the trial the infant's body was exhumed to check whether the brown paper, which had a distinctive blue lining, was the same as some burned at the mill following Read's arrest. The evidence was inconclusive.

However, the case opened in Liverpool amid intense speculation, on 23 November 1893. Spectators watched as the two prisoners stepped forward to the dock. Read seemed slightly nervous but self-possessed. His hair and beard were neatly trimmed and he wore a tightly-buttoned dark blue overcoat. Elizabeth Ann, on the other hand, dressed in a jacket and hat, was highly distressed. She buried her tear-swollen face in a handkerchief, weeping loudly when the letter from her former fiancé was read out.

Throughout the trial Read rose frequently from his seat and leaned on the rails of the dock. He appeared at ease and assured of his freedom as the witnesses presented their statements. The *Burnley Express* remarked on his apparently carefree demeanour:

> *So self-possessed was he that once, at least, he actually joined in the smile and laugh which some trifling incident caused in Court. Throughout his case his bearing was in very marked contrast to that of the girl.*

A look of intense relief passed over Read's face as the judge concluded that, despite a compelling cross-examination by Detective Caminada, the evidence was not sufficient to convict either of the defendants. Ashworth Read and Elizabeth Ann Remington were discharged and left the court together to the hearty congratulations of their friends and family, including Mrs Read, who welcomed her husband with open arms. The following day Ashworth Read resumed his work on the trading floor at the Royal Exchange. Once the rumour of his presence spread, a crowd of heckling businessmen chased him from the building. As recalled by Caminada: 'This was, probably, one of the most remarkable scenes that ever took place on 'Change'.

Infant deaths from natural causes were commonplace in Victorian England, with particularly high mortality rates in the cities. Therefore, it was rare for the circumstances of a child's death to be considered suspicious. The exact number of children killed deliberately is unknown, but as Adrian Gray quotes in *Crime and Criminals of Victorian England*, in 1864, 2,305 deaths of children under one year old were due to unspecified causes and between 1863 and 1887 63 per cent of murders were of infants.

The situation was even more precarious for illegitimate children who, like the child of Ashworth Read and Elizabeth Ann Remington, were generally seen as a burden for their unmarried parents. Many single women who gave birth would be cast out from their family and left to fend for themselves. Shunned by society, their options were very limited: entering the workhouse; starvation on the streets; or giving their child over to the care of a dubious and often ruthless baby farmer. Employers would not hire domestic servants with babies and women who worked in mills and factories had to leave their infants at home. Farmed out, these poor mites were often subjected to neglect, abuse and, in the worst cases, murder. Some illegitimate children died and were disposed of without their births ever being registered; it was as though they had never existed.

This disregard for infants was reinforced in law: infanticide did not exist as a separate offence and defendants could only be tried under a charge of wilful murder which, as a capital offence carried the death penalty. Juries were very reluctant to convict, except on the strongest evidence. From the 1860s, executions for the murder of young children were very rare and female offenders were usually charged with concealment of birth, which carried a much more lenient punishment, with a maximum sentence of two years. It was not surprising therefore that Read and Remington were acquitted of the murder of their child in Blackley Woods. However, Detective Caminada would investigate another questionable infant death with a similar beginning but a very different outcome.

A young lad was playing football with his brother on waste ground near Ashton Canal, just outside Manchester city centre. When he went to wash his boots the boy spotted the legs of a child sticking up from the water. He pulled out the body to discover that it was a female infant, fully dressed, and with a piece of cord tied tightly around her neck. Heavy stones had been attached to the child's waist to weigh her down: this was a clear case of infanticide. The inquest confirmed that the baby was around three months old and she had been in the water for between one and four days.

All attempts by the police to identify the baby proved fruitless, until the widespread publicity of the case yielded some positive leads. Detective Caminada headed the enquiry and before long a lodging-house keeper came forward to identify the child's clothing. The infant's parents had been staying with Mrs French in central Manchester under the name of 'Mr and

Mrs Hirst'. About a month after their arrival Mrs Hirst was confined in the maternity hospital and then returned with a child, whom she called Maud. Baby Maud was baptised in St Luke's Church, Chorlton-on-Medlock. Her parents were Joseph Hirst, 26, a bricklayer and his wife Martha, aged 20, a laundress. Despite their respectable veneer, it did not take long for Caminada to uncover the truth: Joseph Hirst was a violent man who mistreated his wife.

One day the landlady, Mrs French, heard a scream from their room, after which the Hirsts went out. They returned without the baby, explaining that they had left her with her grandmother in Stockport. Three days later Maud's body was found in the canal. Detective Caminada located the grandmother in Stockport and discovered that the couple were not married and that the child's mother was actually called Martha Goddard. Keeping the grandmother's house under surveillance in case Martha returned, he tracked the putative father to another property nearby. When he sent a colleague disguised as a vagrant to the house, he found that the suspect was in fact Hirst's brother, John, who confided to the undercover officer that Joseph was wanted for child murder.

Joseph Hirst was finally arrested in Leicester, after Caminada entered his house in the early hours of the morning and handcuffed him, while he was still sleeping. The detective then located Martha Goddard and took the pair back to Manchester to be charged with the wilful murder of their daughter. In her statement Martha confirmed that she had been the victim of abuse by her partner, which was corroborated by a medical examination. She had left the child alone with Hirst and when she returned Maud was dead. When Caminada confronted him with the allegations, Hirst admitted his guilt: 'I own to it all. I don't expect any pity; the thing is too bad'.

Martha Ann Goddard was acquitted of murder, but Joseph Hirst was found guilty and received the death sentence. He was executed on 3 August 1896 within the precincts of Strangeways Prison. At a quarter to eight in the morning, a crowd of 500 people had gathered outside the gaol in front of the flagstaff, where the black flag would be raised after the execution. Soon after the prison clock struck eight, the sound of the falling of the trap door could be heard, which signalled that the hanging had taken place. The black flag was hoisted up the pole, where it fluttered in the breeze as the crowd carried on their journey to work. It was the first time in Caminada's career of almost 30 years that an investigation had ended on the scaffold.

Detective Caminada was involved in a number of murder cases, but most of them did not result in convictions. In 1889 he had apprehended the prime suspect in the murder of a pawnbroker's assistant in Atherton, near Wigan, but it was a case of mistaken identity and another man was later hanged for the crime. Two years later Scotland Yard enlisted Caminada's help to investigate the Kentish Town and Marylebone murders, which involved the deaths of two women. Although Caminada arrested the suspect, he was later discharged due to insufficient evidence. The real killer was never found. Other cases included the murder of a man in Angel Meadow during a domestic argument, who died of shock when an oil lamp was thrown at him, and the mysterious death of a woman who was hurled down a warehouse lift. Both investigations ended inconclusively.

During Detective Caminada's long police career, he investigated relatively few suspicious deaths. Murder was much less common than other crimes and in 1892 the annual report of the Registrar General recorded that, out of 32,524 inquests into sudden death in England and Wales, only 76 were committed to trial for wilful murder. The only murder cases that Caminada included in his memoirs were the two incidents of infanticide described above.

Chapter Seventeen

'A Chronicle of Crime' (1895–1899)

We have in our police reports realism pushed to its extreme limits, and yet the result is, it must be confessed, neither fascinating nor artistic.
(Sir Arthur Conan Doyle, *A Case of Identity*, 1891)

Sherlock Holmes's scathing attack on the quality of the writing within police accounts encapsulates the rivalry between the authors of detective fiction and real-life detectives who wrote their memoirs, towards the end of the nineteenth century. In the 1880s, stories about imaginary super-sleuths from the pens of writers such as Wilkie Collins, Edgar Allan Poe and the legendary Sir Arthur Conan Doyle, increased in popularity. The appearance of Sherlock Holmes in 1887 established a genre that remains fashionable to the present day. Like modern readers, the Victorians were hooked on the unravelling of mysteries, the solving of crimes and the literary heroes who outwitted dangerous criminals.

Following on from the spate of mid-century detective novels written in the form of memoirs, detective fiction presented the private inquiry agent as a 'sleuth-hound': powerful, brilliant and infallible. With Sherlock Holmes as the epitome of the hero-detective they tracked deadly criminals, exposing their nefarious crimes and dastardly wrongdoings. By comparison the police were presented as mediocre, often inept and nearly always limited in vision and ingenuity: 'Inspector Gregory, to whom the case has been committed, is an extremely competent officer. Were he but gifted with imagination he might rise to great heights in his profession', quipped Sherlock Holmes in *Silver Blaze* (1892).

The unflattering portrayal of police detectives in detective fiction inspired a new trend in real-life law enforcers publishing their memoirs to give a realistic insight into their work. Most early memoirs were written by detectives from the Metropolitan Police, notably from Scotland Yard. In Manchester Superintendent James Bent published his memoirs in 1891, after 42 years in the Lancashire Constabulary. Detective Chief Inspector Jerome Caminada soon followed suit.

In February 1895, Caminada announced the imminent publication of his memoirs in the press. The *Birmingham Daily Post* anticipated that the book 'should make racy and instructive reading'. Purchase was by subscription only and potential readers were required to sign up for a copy in advance at Sherratt & Hughes Bookshop in St Ann's Square. The price was 10s 6d (about £30 today). By comparison, the first edition of *The Adventures of Sherlock Holmes* had been published three years earlier for six shillings. In spite of the high cost, Caminada's publisher, John Heywood, was so overwhelmed with orders that printing had to be delayed.

Twenty-Five Years of Detective Life by Jerome Caminada was typical of the emerging genre. Based on 50 cases, 'dealing with all manner of crime and criminals', the main focus was the modus operandi of the villains that he had encountered in his daily work and the daring exploits he undertook to put them behind bars. A self-made man from a working class background, Caminada was the quintessential author-detective of the time, benefiting from the trend within the publishing industry that sought to engage the interest of a wider market of newly literate potential readers. Furthermore, it was an opportunity to counteract the negative image of police officers portrayed in detective fiction. In the preface to the first volume, he challenged the preconceptions reinforced by Sherlock Holmes:

> *the stories related in the following pages – unlike so many of the so-called stories of detectives – are founded on facts, and are, from first to last, and in all their details, truthful histories of the crimes they purport to describe, and of the detection and punishment of the criminals.*

There is very little information within the memoirs about Caminada's personal life, which was characteristic of their type. These were histories of work, rather than stories about domestic arrangements. The main purpose was to prove the efficiency, skills, intelligence and dogged determination of real operatives in their daily battle with criminals. In addition, Caminada sought to give his readers a vivid insight into the nature of his city, dating from when he first started out on the beat.

During his three decades in the police force, Manchester had begun to change: the slums had been cleared by the construction of the railways, standards of living had improved due to social legislation and crime was decreasing, thanks to a more efficient and extensive police force. Caminada's valuable contribution was recognised by the *Manchester Courier*: 'It is not too much to say that his name is now a "household word," although in certain haunts it is not received with welcome'. Despite these improvements, poverty was still a harsh reality for many and Caminada gave a voice to the dispossessed, by describing their unbearable living conditions in evocative detail. Unashamed of his poverty-stricken childhood, he used his knowledge to instruct the more comfortable inhabitants of Manchester about how the other half lived, exhorting them to be sympathetic to their less fortunate neighbours: 'let us tone down our horror into pity, and in every observation that we make let mercy temper justice'.

Dubbed in the *Daily Despatch* 'a very outspoken book', Caminada's depiction of the sordid alleyways and slums of the recent past was well received by the press. Readers were fascinated by his revelations: 'Mr Caminada has done more than let daylight into the dark avenues of crime' and his 'chronicle of crime' was praised by reviewers as 'a permanent memorial of outward and visible changes in the city' (*Manchester Courier*).

It was usual for police memoirs to be published after detectives had retired, but when the first volume of his memoirs was released in 1895, Caminada was still a serving police officer. In the years that followed his literary success, the force that he served so diligently would be rocked to its very foundations by a series of startling scandals that led to an inquiry by the Home Office.

On 21 November 1896, two cases of 'keeping a disorderly house' (brothel) were brought before Manchester Police Court, which would have a dramatic and lasting impact on the city's police. The defendants were Mary Potton, responsible for a lodging-house of ill repute in Shepley Street, as well as Thomas and Frances Burns, who lived in Lower Ormond Street. Both premises were near the slums of Angel Meadow. A man named William Taylor was also wanted in connection with the first case, but he had absconded, so only the case involving the Burnses proceeded.

Detective Caminada had known Mr and Mrs Burns for more than 30 years. Frances Burns had previously been convicted of pickpocketing at Whaite's Bazaar in central Manchester and her husband had served time for a hotel robbery. The last time that Caminada had crossed their path was in 1889, whilst chasing thieves through Zurich, Berlin and Paris. He had followed his quarry back to London, where he visited a temperance hotel run by Thomas and Frances Burns. After the international thief had been arrested, the Burnses were accused by the criminal fraternity in London of informing the police and forced to flee the capital. On their arrival back in Manchester they opened a refreshment house in Ardwick and soon after, Caminada helped them to acquire a broker's licence. When suspicions first arose that Thomas Burns was keeping a disorderly house, Caminada had investigated, but Burns had assured him that he was merely taking in theatrical lodgers. By the time they were arrested again in 1896 several police officers were also implicated in their illicit activities and a trail of misconduct was uncovered which led back to Superintendent Bannister of D Division.

William Bannister had been promoted to this senior position in 1882, when he was aged just 30, and after only 11 years in the police force. His appointment caused considerable controversy amongst his colleagues, leading them to conclude that he had powerful friends on the watch committee, especially as the protests of the chief constable had been overruled. In Caminada's view, this was where the trouble began: 'This rapid promotion, made over the heads of older officers, was a false step, and the starting point on the road that proved his ruin'.

By 1893, complaints were coming in about Bannister's dubious behaviour. He was seen regularly frequenting the many houses of ill repute located in D Division and it was common knowledge that he was having an illicit relationship with Julia Davis, who kept the Falstaff Inn in Hulme. The chief constable ordered Caminada to investigate, and his findings resulted in an inquiry by the watch committee. Bannister claimed that Davis was merely a family friend and although Chief Constable Wood wanted the watch committee to ask for Bannister's resignation they declined, giving him a reprimand instead.

Superintendent Bannister was seemingly invincible; he would stop at nothing to protect his position and advance his career. In 1895 when Reverend John Kelty gave information to the watch committee that Bannister had been observed in the company of prostitutes and under the influence of drink, the superintendent denied all charges and the case was dismissed. Keen to exact revenge, Bannister brought an action against Kelty, for defamation of character. Later that year Bannister's relationship with Julia Davis was confirmed, when she applied for a renewal of her licence for the Two Terriers beerhouse. The watch committee objected, so Bannister paid for the removal of the key witness to the Isle of Man by one of his officers, until the objection was removed and the licence granted. Superintendent Bannister was heading for a fall and the brothels of Shepley Street would bring an end to his meteoric career.

When Sarah Wilson, proprietress of one of the Shepley Street houses, died in October 1896, William Bannister was among her beneficiaries.

This prompted Sergeant Henscoe, also of D Division, to initiate a covert investigation against his superior officer. On 20 November, Henscoe was granted a warrant for the arrest of William Taylor and Mary Potton, who had taken over the house after Wilson's death. Taylor disappeared and five days later, Bannister withdrew the warrant. When the matter was placed before the police court, a sordid tale of corruption came to light. Aware that trouble was brewing for Taylor, Superintendent Bannister had sent a warning to him via Julia Davis. Taylor had fled while Bannister removed the warrant. Shortly after, Caminada arrested the fugitive Taylor in Birkenhead.

A special meeting of the watch committee was convened at the beginning of December to enquire into the matter, by which time Bannister had resigned his position, claiming that the frequent attacks on his professional life were undermining his health. The Lord Mayor asked Caminada to investigate the connections between the police officers in D Division and the brothels of Shepley Street. He reported that Sarah Wilson had left all her interest in her properties to Bannister, who had been a frequent visitor with William Taylor. The watch committee accepted Bannister's resignation, but withheld his pension in light of the recent charges. As usual Bannister denied the accusations, arguing that his relationship with Taylor was purely of a business nature and that he had withdrawn the warrant for his arrest to place it in more capable hands.

The citizens of Manchester were outraged by the watch committee's decision not to prosecute the ex-superintendent and after further enquiries, a warrant for Bannister's arrest for conspiracy and neglect of duty was finally granted. On 30 December 1896, Caminada arrested Bannister and his lover, Julia Davis and they were brought before the stipendiary. The chief constable instructed Detective Caminada to lead the prosecution.

After stating the facts, Caminada expressed his reluctance to proceed with the charge of conspiracy as, in his opinion, Bannister had already received a severe punishment in the withdrawal of his police pension. After almost 26 years of service, Bannister would have been entitled to around £190 a year. With an invalid wife, a daughter in delicate health and three young sons to support, he was already facing a considerable struggle during the years ahead. The stipendiary, Mr Headlam, overruled Caminada's plea for clemency and ordered him to proceed with the prosecution. In the end, the charge of conspiracy was dismissed due to insufficient evidence and Bannister was convicted of neglect of duty, for which he was fined £10 and his legal costs.

This result still did not satisfy the public and complaints against Bannister and the officers of D Division escalated. Caminada took charge of the investigation and soon became embroiled in accusations of corruption. The scandals reached fever pitch and pressure from the public forced the watch committee to request the Home Secretary to launch an official inquiry. Sir Matthew White Ridley appointed Mr S. J. Dugdale QC, Recorder of Birmingham to conduct a thorough investigation into the Manchester City Police Force.

The Home Office Inquiry began on 24 May 1897, casting a bright light into the dark goings-on of D Division. There were many brothels and beerhouses within the jurisdiction of the division. Some had been closed, but many remained open, notably the houses in Shepley Street. The investigation confirmed that Superintendent Bannister had been in league with the owners, warning them when they were being watched or when summonses were taken out against them. Furthermore, he had actively encouraged actions against rival brothels.

The officers of D Division were reluctant to make complaints against Bannister, as they knew there would be serious consequences. In one recorded case an inspector had complained about the conduct of one of Bannister's loyal officers and he had been 'banished' to a remote part of the division as punishment. Superintendent Bannister had ruled his division through intimidation and even during the course of the inquiry, many of his faithful colleagues supported him by making accusations against other officers, including Detective Caminada, who was called to answer a charge of owning a beerhouse. Caminada admitted that he had been the proprietor of the Shepherd's Bush, subject to a lease that he had purchased with some cottages and as soon as the lease expired he had sold it. The judge was satisfied with his explanation. Other baseless accusations were brought against the detective, but they were dismissed as 'frivolous' and born of jealousy.

The Recorder of Birmingham concluded that D Division of the Manchester City Police was in a state of disarray, with morale and discipline at an all-time low. However, the other four divisions, including E Division where Caminada worked, were operating efficiently. By the end of the inquiry a number of officers from D Division had already resigned or been transferred and a new superintendent appointed. The whole affair was a turning point in the history of the police force in Manchester.

On 2 December 1897 Jerome Caminada was promoted to the position of Superintendent of E Division, on a salary of £290 per annum (the equivalent of roughly £27,000 today, but a considerable salary at the time). After surviving one of the most far-reaching investigations into the Manchester Police, he was rewarded for his loyalty and conduct.

Despite his exoneration by the inquiry, one of the main victims of the scandals was Chief Constable Charles Malcolm Wood, who had succeeded Captain William Palin in 1881. The son of a civil servant, Wood had grown up in India, where he had joined the Indian Civil Service after leaving school. He rose to the position of District Superintendent of the Sind Police in Karachi, but when he was appointed Chief Constable in Manchester, he was a stranger to the city and unaccustomed to the ways of the British police force. Inevitably, his term of office was tainted by the Bannister scandal and Wood was accused of turning a blind eye to the excesses of D Division. After suffering vehement attacks from the press, his health began to decline and he resigned his post on 26 January 1898, with a full pension of £500 a year.

Superintendent Caminada must have been devastated by this decision as he was firmly committed to his superior officer, even dedicating his memoirs to him: 'I cannot here attempt to express to Mr Charles Malcolm Wood, the Chief Constable of Manchester, the thanks I owe him, or my gratitude for his uniform and unbroken consideration and kindness'. (It is also likely that Caminada had named his son after Wood.) Contemporary commentators suggested that Caminada never recovered from the loss of his close ally on the force and that he suffered under the new regime because of his loyalty to the former chief constable. His increasingly tenuous position was exacerbated by the temporary appointment of the new Acting Chief-Constable, William Fell Smith, with whom his relationship had been soured by the banned Slattery lecture.

A year later on 5 January 1899, Jerome Caminada resigned his post as Superintendent of the Manchester City Police Force. Despite the unpleasant revelations of the police scandal, his illustrious career remained untarnished until the end. In 1895 he had received personal recommendations from the Postmaster General and the Duke of Norfolk for his contribution to the conviction of several people for telegraph frauds. Shortly after, the watch committee had rewarded him for the apprehension of 1,225 offenders. Furthermore, in his role as superintendent, he had obtained an increase in pay for his colleagues in E Division, who had presented him with a set of fine ivory-handled cutlery as a mark of their esteem.

When Caminada's retirement was announced, the press celebrated his achievements. The *Evening Telegraph* called him 'one of the most noted detectives of the country, a man of whom Manchester has been pardonably proud'. Dubbed a 'terror to evil doers', the article praised his special qualities as a police detective:

> *His career has been one of the most remarkable and brilliant in police annals. Probably no man living knows more about crime and criminals, their habits and habitats, their cunning and duplicity.*

After 31 years of service Detective Caminada received a pension of £210 per annum, almost his full salary, and £15 more than his official entitlement. The first task he undertook after his retirement was to write a second volume of memoirs.

Chapter Eighteen

State Secrets and Undercover Missions
(1901)

The census taken on 31 March 1901 shows Detective Caminada and his family living in Denmark Road, on the boundary of Chorlton-on-Medlock and Moss Side. An affluent part of the city close to Manchester University, his immediate neighbours included several doctors, a dentist, a cotton merchant and an engineer. Next-door lived photographer Warwick Brookes, who took Caminada's picture for the *Police Review* in 1898. Opposite the Caminadas' home was Whitworth Park, occupying 18 acres. Home to Whitworth Art Gallery, it opened to the public in 1890, boasting a boating lake and pleasant walks.

Jerome Caminada, aged 57, was living in these agreeable surroundings with his wife, Amelia and 10-year-old daughter, Mary. They had a domestic servant, Margaret O'Brien, 35, from Ireland. Their son, Charles, now 13, was boarding at the Roman Catholic Stonyhurst College near Blackburn, where Sir Arthur Conan Doyle had been a pupil 25 years earlier.

After their mother's admittance to the workhouse in the late 1880s, there is no trace in public records of the fate of Jerome's sister, Teresa, and her daughter Annie. In 1901 Caminada's older brother, John Baptiste, was living in the working class district of Cheetham, closer to the city centre. John Baptiste worked from home as a druggist, assisted by his daughter, Florence (also known as Mary), who was then 22. The census revealed that John Baptiste was suffering from paralysis, a possible symptom of the syphilis that had most likely led to his mother's blindness. A year later on 18 August 1902 he died, aged 65, of drink-related disease. Unfortunately, no record of the inquest into his death has survived.

Despite his busy family life and the management of his properties, Caminada published the second volume of his memoirs in the spring of 1901. Although it comprised individual cases like the first, in many ways this volume was quite different. Having clearly been affected by the scandals at the end of his police career, Caminada devoted many pages to explaining these events and justifying his role in the controversy. In addition, he expressed his opinions on prison conditions, the rehabilitation of criminals, juvenile offenders and the organisation of the Manchester Police Force. Heavier in tone and dense in parts, this was a much more serious work. Sold at the same price as the first volume, Caminada said that the positive response of the public to his earlier publication had motivated him to share more of his stories and experiences as a detective.

Yet the recurring theme of the bravery and efficiency of the police throughout the book, perhaps suggests a deeper motive: 'A good policeman, then, requires tact, patience, and courage, qualities for which, it is to be feared, the majority of the public seldom give him credit'. Ever the realist, Caminada is scathing about the 'fanciful pictures' of detective fiction, yet in spite of his disapprobation reviewers could not resist comparing his work to the increasingly popular literary genre. Responses to this volume were varied, but the *Manchester Evening Chronicle* was generally positive: 'This book is considerably more than mere detective stories, imaginative or otherwise'. The article introduces Caminada as a man 'gifted with a personality', highlighting his individuality:

he is not a man to be herded with the average type. He has always his own point of view. It might be right or it might be wrong, but that view is according to the character and temperament of the man. He thinks for himself, and has the courage very often to say what he thinks.

However, the reviewer criticises the structure and style, complaining that the introduction is 'cumbrous' and that Caminada lapses too frequently into emotionalism. It is true that the memoir cannot be classed as 'light reading' and the critic quips that readers would need a strong pair of hands to hold the tome for long enough to digest the contents. The inevitable conclusion is that Caminada writes with 'a policeman's pen' and that his style, although he tells a good story, is not equal to that of a fiction writer: 'He would never do to enter into competition with the author of "Sherlock Holmes"'.

The comparison between detective fiction and real-life detective memoirs permeates reviews in the press. The critique in the *Manchester Guardian* opens with an exposé of the literary disadvantages faced by the author-detective:

In his detective duties he sets out from given facts; he goes on to collect as many facts as possible, and keeping all the facts in his head or his pocket-book – facts relevant and irrelevant alike – he tries to establish with their aid a final fact… So dear are they to him that when he comes to write his story he cannot bring himself to throw them away, and therefore in they go, in flat defiance of literary form and with a merciless disregard of the reader's flagging powers of attention.

According to the reviewer, this adversely affects the narrative style and in the case of Caminada's writing, it 'may seem to the admirers of Sherlock Holmes disappointingly dull and tame'. Taking care to point out all its faults, the article concludes with a cautiously positive view of the memoirs:

And yet in spite of all its faults, its clumsiness of narrative, its exasperating allusiveness, its lack of imagination, its trite moralising, and its reckless attacks upon people who, whatever may be thought of their methods, are disinterestedly trying to do good – in spite of all these blemishes and some others, it is an interesting and even fascinating book.

Despite these mixed reviews, the second volume sold well and was soon available in libraries throughout the country. It was particularly popular as a history of Manchester, and the publisher received many orders from other countries, including India, America and Belgium. Even the Lord Chief Justice was alleged to have read it. However, not everyone appreciated Caminada's literary efforts and three years after its publication he was called upon to defend his work, when a judge criticised the detrimental impact of the book on would-be criminals.

Two young men were charged with burglary in Chester and at the Assizes they claimed that they had been influenced by Caminada's memoirs. The judge added his observations that the 'undesirable character' of the books might cause crime rather than act as a deterrent, and that copies ought to be removed from public libraries. The chairman of the Libraries' Committee condemned the judge's comments, reassuring him that careful selection of titles was rigorously maintained.

In an interview with the *Manchester Courier*, Caminada defended his writing:

Both bishops and judges have complimented me on the work, which is a clean and wholesome book. Editors of newspapers have seen it, Press notices have been published, and in no case up to the present has there been made the slightest complaint.

Jerome Caminada's second volume of memoirs may have been a turgid read, but they exposed a thrilling and well-guarded secret: since the early 1870s the British government had employed him, and other officers, in undercover missions. In the opening paragraphs of the book he divulged that he had tailed suspicious characters, decoded messages and infiltrated secret societies, not only at home but throughout America and continental Europe too. After whetting the appetite of his readers, he states that he is unable to disclose further information about his clandestine activities, in order to protect the identity of his collaborators and preserve national security: 'Such information would also be welcomed and used by the enemies of society. Therefore my readers will see the necessity of keeping it a sealed book, and will excuse me accordingly'.

Despite the need for confidentiality, he revealed the details of one case, when he was instructed to catch a military spy. In 1892 Chief Inspector Caminada received orders from the Solicitor of the Treasury to carry out surveillance of an ex-quartermaster, Edmund Holden, who was living in Hulme, Manchester. A surveyor, Holden had enlisted in the Royal Engineers in 1872 and served in Ireland, Gibraltar and Malta. He had enjoyed rapid promotion in his army career, rising to the rank of company sergeant-major and then quartermaster. In Malta he was in charge of the Draughtsmen's Department and supervised work on the construction of batteries and fortresses on the island, including the Della Grazie Battery above the Grand Harbour.

Holden left Malta in 1891 and returned to England, where he gained a post as Civil Foreman of Works in the Engineers' Department at Parkhurst, Isle of Wight. A year later he was transferred to Curragh Camp, a military training centre in Ireland, from which he was dismissed after fraudulently misappropriating funds. Following his fall from grace, Holden was unable to find further employment in the army. In financial difficulties, he wrote to his former subordinate, Lance-Corporal Thomas McCartney, who was still serving in Malta, asking for information about gun placements in the forts and when McCartney handed the letter to his commanding officer, the warrant for Holden's arrest was issued.

Caminada shadowed the spy in Manchester and then to London, where he arrested him en route to a rendezvous with his contact in Paris. When the detective searched Holden, he found letters and documents in his bag, which, once he had decoded them, enabled him to build a picture of the fugitive's treachery and double-dealing. Later Caminada found several letters at Holden's home from his Parisian correspondent, some with money enclosed for trips to the French capital. One letter asked for tracings of the positions of guns and their capability on the island of Malta. On another occasion Holden had written to McCartney for up-to-date technical details to send to his foreign paymaster. Detective Caminada had conclusive proof that Holden had been selling information about the calibre and positions of arms to the French, which could have posed a threat to British security in the event of war.

Edmund Holden, 42, was charged under the Official Secrets Act of 1889 with having attempted to procure Thomas McCartney to be guilty of a breach of official trust. He was found guilty and sentenced to 12 months' imprisonment for 'a very bad and dangerous offence'. Detective Caminada had captured his spy: 'Next to betraying one's country into the hands of an enemy, there is no crime so abhorrent to the patriotic man as that of divulging the military secrets of one's own people, and playing the spy for a rival power'. Throughout his career, Caminada played the role of spy himself in undercover missions for the Home Office, as he tracked first Fenians and later anarchists, but true to his word he never revealed the extent of his covert operations.

In the early 1880s there was growing unrest amongst the working population. In the midst of a deep economic depression, socialist and anarchist groups called for economic and political reform, attracting the attention of the police. At the same time, Irish nationalism was gathering pace on the mainland and police officers were regularly shadowing suspects. The Criminal Investigation Department had been established in 1878, headed by Superintendent Frederick Adolphus 'Dolly' Williamson. When the Fenians launched the dynamite campaign, with the explosion at Salford Infantry Barracks in 1881, the detectives of Scotland Yard and their colleagues throughout the country began to gather intelligence in earnest.

As the bombing of public buildings increased, the murder of Lord Cavendish and Thomas Burke in Dublin instigated the founding of the Irish Branch in March 1883. Under the supervision of Williamson, the Irish Branch (later known as the Special Branch) procured the services of other uniformed and plain-clothes officers to suppress acts of terrorism by tracking Fenian suspects, as they passed through Britain. They were particularly keen to recruit officers from an Irish Roman Catholic background and Detective Caminada fitted the profile perfectly.

Dolly Williamson was the protégé of Detective Inspector Jonathan Whicher, famous for his investigation into the Road Hill House murder in 1860. Williamson rose through the ranks to the position of Chief

Superintendent of Scotland Yard in 1881 and was still in charge during the case of the 'Jack the Ripper' murders in the late 1880s. When the former Chief Superintendent of the Birmingham Force, James Black, died in 1926 his obituary revealed an interesting and previously unknown connection: the *Western Daily Express* printed that when Williamson was asked how many real detectives he knew, he replied, 'I know only three: they are Black of Birmingham, Jerome Caminada of Manchester, and one of my own men'.

It is likely, therefore, that Caminada worked directly for Williamson under the auspices of the Special Branch. The fact that his superior officer, Chief Constable Wood was commended by the Home Office reinforces the probability, although it is unclear exactly how Caminada earned Williamson's respect. Further evidence is provided by the survival of two telegrams, now held in the Greater Manchester Police Museum and Archives, which were sent to Caminada from Wood whilst he was on special duty in Le Havre; one recalling him to Britain and the other instructing him to await further instructions from the Home Office.

By 1901 Jerome Caminada was no longer undertaking secret missions for the British government but his 'life of crowded adventure', as alluded to in the *Daily Mail*, continued undiminished. In his roles as city councillor and private detective he would remain a frequent visitor to the law courts for the following decade – on both sides of the bench.

Chapter Nineteen

'The Garibaldi of Detectives'
(1902–1914)

Mr Caminada is still a comparatively young man full of vigour and energy.
(*Evening Telegraph*, 7 January 1899)

W hen Jerome Caminada retired at the age of 54, he continued to lead an active life, in the zealous and diligent manner that had characterised his 30-year-long police career. His commitment to his home city of Manchester remained as steadfast as ever and his fight to clean up the streets carried on unabated.

In the early 1880s, when he and his wife were living in Old Trafford at the beginning of their marriage, Caminada had begun acquiring properties. In addition to the cottages and public house revealed to be in his ownership during the police scandals of the late 1890s, he had also bought land in Chorlton-on-Medlock, where he eventually settled with his family. By 1902 the ex-detective had acquired a considerable portfolio of property, an occupation that would take him into the courtroom several times, to protect his interests.

Just after his resignation in January 1899, Caminada brought an action against a construction company for breach of contract. He had paid £1,750 (worth just over £160,000 today) for the building of four houses in Chorlton-on-Medlock. As agreed, when the work was completed he had paid the contractors in full, but shortly afterwards the plaster had started to blister.

Using his knowledge of the law, Caminada sued the firm for damages. The defendants explained that they had used old bricks, with Caminada's agreement, and this had caused the problem. At the hearing, despite concluding that the dispute could have been settled by a professional builder rather than an expensive court case, the judge awarded the former police officer damages of £75.

By the early 1900s Caminada had added to his growing property business with the purchase of houses in Richmond Street in central Manchester, near to the Bridgewater Canal. The next time he appeared in court was to bring a suit against the proprietors of a warehouse, claiming that the unloading of their 'lurries' (horse drawn lorries) was causing an obstruction of the pavement for his tenants. The firm would place four men along the footpath, who threw parcels to each other from the lorry to the warehouse's loading bay. Considering this to be very dangerous, Caminada cited the case of a gentleman having been struck by a parcel, which knocked off his hat. He further complained that sometimes two lines of men were formed and lorries backed up to the warehouse over the pavement. As usual, the experienced prosecutor won his case and the company incurred a fine.

Despite his lucrative business interests, Caminada was not ready to relinquish his detective work and, in keeping with the contemporary trend amongst retired senior police officers, he established his own private inquiry agency.

In *The Sign of the Four* (1890), Sherlock Holmes pronounced that he was the 'only unofficial consulting detective' in the country. In the realm of fiction, when police detectives and private inquiry agents failed to solve baffling cases, they turned to Holmes for help. In reality Jerome Caminada had no such recourse when he was working as a detective, either in the police or in his private practice. He had to rely on his own expert knowledge, exceptional memory and powers of deduction but as he would soon discover, this was more difficult outside the protection of the force.

The latter years of the nineteenth century saw a rise in private detective agencies. Employed police officers often engaged in private work as a sideline and detectives set up their own agency after retiring. Former police detectives had the advantage of their contacts in the criminal justice system, the press and on the streets. Like Caminada they already had a considerable network of informers, as well as former colleagues inside the force, with whom they often collaborated, by taking on assignments that the police were less keen to pursue. At the height of Sherlock Holmes's popularity, the worlds of fact and fiction merged more closely for Caminada, as he joined the ranks of private detectives. However, the reality was far less glamorous than life at 221b Baker Street.

In April 1902 Caminada was back in court, but this time he was in the dock charged with trespass and assault. A 'gentleman of very considerable position', named Mr Tunnicliffe, engaged him in connection with a divorce proceeding brought by his wife, Elizabeth Maud Tunnicliffe. When the couple had married in December 1899, the groom enjoyed a high social position, but by contrast his bride 'had not led an absolutely virtuous life'. Despite their apparent differences, the newly-weds settled near the

University of Manchester, where they remained until their marriage failed in August 1901. After the split Elizabeth rented a small house with the financial support of two lodgers. She also employed a servant, Eliza Morgan.

Later that year, Elizabeth Tunnicliffe filed for divorce on the grounds of adultery. In his defence, her estranged husband accused her of the same offence and employed Caminada to gather evidence. On the morning of 17 February 1902, Elizabeth's servant, Eliza Morgan, left the house to buy some milk for coffee. While she was absent, a man named Stanton and a young solicitor's clerk slipped in through the open door and made their way straight to the bedroom of one of the lodgers, named Mulliner. They threatened Mulliner, who had a previous conviction for larceny, and all three men left. When Eliza returned, she was about to rush upstairs to tell her mistress about the intrusion when there was a knock at the door.

The two men had returned with Caminada and, pushing the young girl to one side, they ran up the stairs to Elizabeth Tunnicliffe's bedroom, where they found her alone in her nightdress, lying on the bed. Apparently Caminada said, 'Oh, you have just got out of the other bed', intimating that she had been sleeping in Mulliner's bed. She called him a liar, to which he replied, 'Get up out of this: you are used to this kind of thing'. Unable to find evidence of adultery, Caminada and his associates left.

Outraged by the intrusion, Mrs Tunnicliffe brought the action against Caminada for his behaviour towards her. During an adjournment in the hearing, the two parties reached a settlement and Elizabeth Tunnicliffe withdrew the case. However, during the prosecution, an interesting point was raised about the ex-police officer's involvement in the case. The plaintiff's solicitor had remarked that Caminada, as a private inquiry agent, had to undertake 'irregular' activities to gain evidence. He suggested that Caminada's long experience in the police force had left him with little regard for the manner in which he conducted his private work: 'the more zealous a gentleman was in that line the more difficult were very often the positions in which he found himself when doing work for the public'.

The following year Caminada was back in court on similar charges. In July 1903, Sion Levy filed a suit of unlawful wounding against the detective, who had been acting on behalf of Levy's former employer, Abdullah Elias, a wealthy ship merchant. The long running saga had begun a year earlier, when Levy had accused Elias of assault, while he was in his employ as a clerk. Elias and his colleague, Eliahoo Joseph, both originally from Baghdad, had explained that they had been forced to remove Levy from their property in a case of trespass. The jury had found for Levy and he had received damages.

Abdullah Elias was a successful businessman and prominent member of the Jewish community in Manchester. During the case brought against him by his former employee, he had instructed Caminada to collect information about the plaintiff. It was during this work that Levy alleged that Caminada had entered his house and struck him a blow to the head with a piece of wood saying, 'I will kill you before you can give evidence'. Once again, during the adjournment, Sion Levy withdrew his complaint. He was later convicted of conspiracy to give false evidence.

As Detective Caminada discovered, the nature of private inquiries was much more ambiguous than the crimes investigated by the police, perhaps due to their often personal nature. The private detective was inextricably drawn into bitter divorces, complex relationships and vendettas, which may have been the reason why Caminada made the decision to launch a political career instead.

In October 1907 Jerome Caminada presented himself for nomination as an Independent candidate, to represent the Openshaw Ward on the Manchester City Council. At the hustings in Whitworth Hall he vowed to stand for the ratepayers of Openshaw, especially in relation to the mismanagement of the Manchester Corporation. According to the *Manchester Guardian*, the meeting was 'somewhat lively' and Caminada was interrupted several times by the rowdy crowd. He stood his ground and the resolution was passed that he was a 'fit and proper' potential representative, even though 'many hands were held up against it'. A Labour candidate, Joseph Bevir Williams, secretary of the Amalgamated Musicians' Union, was also selected.

Openshaw is two miles east of Manchester, on the other side of the city from where Caminada lived. A manufacturing district, it had experienced a massive population explosion during the nineteenth century, with as many as 20,000 inhabitants during the later decades. Heavy industry had replaced the traditional cottage bleaching trade and it was the site of important engineering works, notably the gun–making factory of Armstrong Whitworth, a major arms supplier during the First World War. The district was also known for radical politics and was home to supporters of socialism and trade unionism.

Strongly opposed to socialism, Jerome Caminada canvassed for votes as a trade unionist. Billing himself as a 'practical man' and a 'friend and neighbour', he pledged to use his pragmatism and no–nonsense attitude to gain the support of local residents. As reported in the *Daily Despatch*, Caminada was once the secretary of a trade union and during a public meeting, he was beset by socialists, who demanded his credentials. Under attack he produced a book confirming his membership of the trade union, which he triumphantly passed around the audience. At the election he won by a large majority and was duly appointed to take his seat on the Manchester City Council.

For the following three years Caminada was actively involved in council business, as well as serving on several committees. His time as a city councillor was characterised by his criticism of the organisation of the police force and advocacy of economy in council spending.

Furthermore, Caminada engaged in many charitable works and one particularly poignant campaign concerned a young man, who had lost his life while trying to save that of another. John Amos McAvoy, 24, was a window cleaner living in Richmond Street, possibly in one of the houses owned by Caminada. Living close to the Bridgewater Canal, the family kept a lifebuoy and grappling irons on hand for the regular occasions when people fell into the water. In July 1907 some young boys were bathing in the canal when one fell in, whilst filling a water pistol.

The alarm was raised and John McAvoy jumped in to rescue him. After previously having saved many other people from drowning, tragically he died in the attempt. Three onlookers dived in and rescued the boy, who had panicked and pulled McAvoy under the water. The young lad survived and was 'apparently little the worse for his immersion' (*Manchester Courier*). Jerome Caminada formed a small committee to raise funds for a memorial stone to mark John's grave in Southern Cemetery, as well as some money for his bereaved parents. He wrote several letters to the local press to solicit subscribers, so that 'the heroic but unrecorded deeds which he accomplished should not pass unnoticed'.

In 1910, at the end of his first term on the council, Jerome Caminada sought re-election, advocating lower rates and fair competition in the awarding of municipal contracts. His opponent was Labour candidate, G. F. Titt. The outcome of the election was a dead-heat between the two, each receiving exactly 1,482 votes. In an unprecedented move, the returning officer cast the deciding vote against Caminada and he lost his seat. He did not stand again.

Jerome Caminada was recorded on the 1911 census as living with his wife in the large nine-roomed family house in Denmark Road, where he would remain for the rest of his life. His son, Charles aged 23, had taken on the family property business and was still living at home, along with his sister, Mary, 20. On the evening of the census, family friend Mary McCann was visiting the Caminadas. A 66-year-old unmarried woman also from Manchester, she was Mary's godmother.

At the age of 67, Caminada had retired from active work at last, but there would be one more major court case before he could enjoy a quieter life.

Recovering from an attack of diabetes in September 1911, Jerome Caminada was enjoying a weekend alone in Rhyl, North Wales, when he paid three shillings for a day trip to Llanfair, about 30 miles further along the coast. The tour was by charabanc, a horse-drawn coach popular in the early twentieth century for outings and pleasure trips. Pulled by four horses the vehicle was at full capacity, with 22 passengers on four long seats.

On the return journey the passengers complained about the speed of the coach, but the driver paid them no heed, egged on by a group of young lads, who were singing merrily and ringing a bell. After the rapid descent of a steep hill, one of the wheels slipped onto a grassy patch and the coach overturned, spilling its load of day-trippers into the road. Caminada was thrown out of the vehicle, losing consciousness as he hit the ground. His nose and some of his ribs were broken and he was bleeding profusely from a wound to the head.

Two doctors attended to him at the scene of the accident, before transporting him to the Black Lion Public House in Llanfair, where he remained in bed for nine days. Once he had recovered, Caminada returned home to Manchester, but it was another three months before he was able to walk unaided. As soon as he was well enough, the ex-detective initiated a lawsuit for negligence against the proprietors of the coach company, Brookes Brothers, to recover damages for personal injuries and to pay for his nursing care.

At the hearing in March 1912, Caminada's representative maintained that the coach was top-heavy in structure and unsuitable for hilly country, with wide seats that hung up to 17 inches over the sides. An expert confirmed that the undercarriage was very light and the springs too weak for the weight. The driver, 23-year-old Daniel Brookes, stated that the accident had been caused by one of the leading horses shying at a pile of slates at the bottom of the hill. The coach had toppled over as he was trying to regain control of the animals. An experienced driver, Brookes had never had an accident before and he had acted appropriately in the circumstances. Daniel Roberts, the coachbuilder, testified that the charabanc was not top-heavy and that his firm had built 40 similar vehicles, none of which had ever overturned. The jury took just 15 minutes to return a verdict in favour of the defendants. Caminada had lost his final case and his health never fully recovered.

On 10 March 1914, just five days before his seventieth birthday, Jerome Caminada died at his home in Denmark Road. The cause of death was recorded as diabetes (from which he had suffered for six years), influenza and heart disease. Four days later, a Requiem Mass was held for him at the Church of the Holy Name, where he had celebrated his marriage and the baptisms of his children. The renowned detective's funeral was attended by many of the city's dignitaries, including the Lord Mayor, members of the city council, several magistrates and representatives of the various organisations to which he had belonged. His former colleagues also attended to bid their comrade farewell, including ex-Detective Inspector Peter Wilson, who had worked with Caminada on many cases. After the Mass, his funeral cortège of five carriages proceeded to Southern Cemetery, where Jerome was laid to rest in the family grave.

Judge Edward Abbot Parry gave the eulogy at Caminada's funeral. As Judge of Manchester County Court from 1894 to 1911, he had known the detective well, describing him as 'a great character' and 'good citizen'. He also praised his sterling qualities and unorthodox methods, as well as his role as a leader: 'He was a man of resource, energy, and initiative, and he never stultified himself by a petty adherence to office regulations. He was the Garibaldi of detectives'. Furthermore, the judge remembered Caminada's kindness, commenting wryly:

> *What I want to remind my fellow-citizens, now he is gone, is that in all the miserable work he had to do, and did so ably, he was always a human being with a kind heart. He never lost his faith in human nature, though he knew more about moral diseases than most bishops.*

On a more personal note he recalled a poignant moment in their shared history, which had brought them closer together and cemented their friendship: 'One does not readily forget a man who has been near you and done you kindness in the hour of trouble'.

On 26 July 1898 Judge Parry had been presiding over a case against court bailiff, William Taylor, to have his licence revoked for misconduct, which would have meant the loss of Taylor's livelihood. The court was filled to capacity and it had been a busy morning for the judge. When Judge Parry announced that Taylor was unfit to hold a bailiff's licence, the defendant sprang up the steps and jumped onto the bench. Pulling out a revolver, he held it to the judge's head and shot him three times. Judge Parry reeled backwards, his hand covering a wound to his cheek, while his clerk grappled with Taylor and wrestled him to the ground.

As the scene of horror unfolded, the spectators in the public gallery began to scream and there was a mad rush towards the doors. In the struggle at the bench another shot was discharged and a bullet whizzed over the heads of the fleeing crowds. Judge Parry sustained wounds to the neck and face, but fortunately a doctor from the Manchester Royal Infirmary was present in court and he staunched the bleeding with handkerchiefs. Taylor was overpowered and dragged into another room to wait for the police.

Superintendent Caminada was in the detective office when he received news of the attempted assassination of Judge Parry. Grabbing his revolver, he ran out of the office and jumped into a cab, heading straight to the courtroom. On arrival he accompanied the injured judge to a private nursing home and helped him into bed, before returning to the scene of the crime. Taylor was later sentenced to 20 years' penal servitude for attempted murder.

After the shooting Caminada investigated other 'half-mad folk' who sent death threats to the judge and his legal colleagues. Judge Parry recalled one case that revealed the detective's 'slow sense of humour'. Caminada had been interviewing one such letter writer and when he met the judge afterwards, he reported with a sigh:

> It's no good, judge. I've been with the fellow an hour or two and I can't knock any reason into him. He's got hold of the wrong end of the stick, and as I keep telling him: it's not you he wants to shoot at all – it's the registrar.

At the end of the eulogy, Judge Parry gave a moving summary of his colleague and friend: 'All of us in Manchester knew Jerome Caminada's worth as a detective; not everyone knew his honesty, faith, and kindness. May he rest in peace'.

The judge's sentiments were echoed in the many obituaries that appeared in the local and national press. The *Daily Mail* described how Detective Caminada was 'widely known throughout the country for his clever and daring detective work'. Other newspapers reflected on how Caminada's reputation had travelled 'beyond the precincts of the city, and was of great service in the unravelling of many crimes' (*Manchester Courier*). A more personal obituary in the *Daily Despatch* emphasised Caminada's deep sense of charity, faith and loyalty:

In his public life he was absolutely fearless, and never hesitated to back up
his opinions and his principles… He was a man of strong likes and dislikes.
A kindness done to him would never be forgot (sic) and the few people who
were really intimate with him found him a very firm friend. On the other
hand he could be a stern enemy, in his home and family life he presented an
irreproachable example.

Jerome Caminada had provided well for his family throughout his married
life and after his death the gross value of his estate was £16,527 (worth
almost three quarters of a million pounds today). He left all his furniture and
personal possessions to his wife, Amelia, together with an indefinite income
of £10 a week. The remainder of his estate was to be held in trust for his
children and any future dependents. His will also included instructions for
special payments: £1,000 to his nephew, Louis Caminada, the son of John
Baptiste; the same to Stonyhurst College, where his own son had studied;
and smaller amounts to various Catholic and civic charities.

The year after his death, on 9 December 1915, the Caminada family
celebrated the wedding of his daughter, Mary, aged 24, to Herbert Sharp, an
accountant. Six weeks later her brother, Charles Bernard, married Constance
Isabella Cowley. Both weddings were held in the family church of the Holy
Name. The next generation soon followed, with the birth of Jerome Charles
Caminada in 1916, Bernard Sharp in 1918, and Nevil Francis Caminada
in 1925. Jerome's widow, Amelia moved to Southport with her daughter's
family, where she died in 1928.

Throughout Detective Caminada's exceptional career he was often
measured against his imaginary equivalent, and the result was not always
in his favour. After his death the *Manchester Courier* wrote, 'Mr Caminada
was not exactly a Sherlock Holmes, but as a detective he did good service to
Manchester'. The *Manchester Guardian* attempted to counteract this rather
unfair opinion, summing up the differences between the two detectives:

In real life the successful detective is not a man endowed with extraordinary
powers of impersonation and disguise, an expert knowledge of chemistry, and
a brain which has to be kept cool with wet towels, when it is at work, but
rather one who has acquired by slow degrees and after many years of obscure
routine a personal acquaintance at once minute and wide with habitual
criminals.

In *The Sign of the Four*, Sherlock Holmes listed the essential qualities for the ideal detective as the powers of observation and deduction, and knowledge. There is no doubt that Detective Jerome Caminada had all three in abundance and that he exploited his skills to fight crime on the streets of his city for more than three decades. He tackled cunning criminals and solved intriguing crimes, employing methods often as ingenious as Holmes's, but more importantly, his adventures were completely authentic.

His widely publicised cases could easily have provided inspiration for the stories of Sir Arthur Conan Doyle. It is not surprising, therefore, that Detective Caminada should have been compared, both during his lifetime and after his death, to the great Sherlock Holmes, and as Caminada was a man of strong opinions, it is only right that he should have the final word.

> *Fully conscious of the fact that the stories which I have laid before the reader are perhaps crude, and without literary finish, I still venture to submit them as depicting the career of one who for more than a quarter of a century has had much to do with successful detection and punishment of crime as any police-officer in the world.*
>
> (Jerome Caminada, *Twenty-Five Years of Detective Life*,
> Volume II, 1901)

Bibliography

General

Caminada, Jerome, *Twenty-Five Years of Detective Life*, Volume I (John Heywood, 1895)

Caminada, Jerome, *Twenty-Five Years of Detective Life*, Volume II (John Heywood, 1901)

Curtis, Liz, *The Cause of Ireland: From the United Irishmen to Partition* (Beyond the Pale Publications, 1994)

Pritchard, R. E., *Dickens's England: Life in Victorian Times* (The History Press, 2002)

Quinlivan, Patrick and Rose, Paul, *The Fenians in England 1865–1872* (John Calder, 1982)

Rea, Anthony, *Manchester's Little Italy: Memories of the Italian Colony of Ancoats* (Neil Richardson, 1988)

Wade, Stephen, *Spies in the Empire: Victorian Military Intelligence* (Anthem Press, 2007)

Manchester

Bethune Reach, Angus; Aspin Chris, ed. *A Cotton-Fibre Halo: Manchester and the Textile Districts in 1849* (Royd Press, 2007)

Briggs, Asa, *Victorian Cities* (Penguin Books, 1963)

Cooper, Glynis, *The Illustrated History of Manchester's Suburbs* (Breedon Books, 2007)

Davies, Andrew, *The Gangs of Manchester: The Story of the Scuttlers, Britain's First Youth Cult* (Milo Books, 2009)

Engels, Friedrich, *The Condition of the Working-Class in England in 1844* (George Allen & Unwin Ltd, 1892)

Heaton, Frank, *The Manchester Village: Deansgate Remembered* (Neil Richardson, 1995)

Jones, Steve, *Manchester…The Sinister Side* (Wicked Publications, 1997)

Kidd, Alan, *Manchester: A History* (Carnegie Publishing, 2006)

Makepeace, Chris, *Looking Back at Hulme, Moss Side, Chorlton on Medlock & Ardwick* (Willow Publishing, 1995)

O'Neill, Joseph, *Crime City: Manchester's Victorian Underworld* (Milo Books, 2008)

Phillips Kay-Shuttleworth, Sir James, *The Moral and Physical Condition of the Working Classes, Employed in the Cotton Manufacture in Manchester* (James Ridgeway, 1832)

Thomson, W.H., *History of Manchester to 1852* (John Sherratt and Son, 1966)

Crime and punishment

Chesney, Kellow, *The Victorian Underworld* (Penguin Books, 1991, 3rd edition)

Dell, Simon, *The Victorian Policeman* (Shire Publications, 2004)

Gray, Adrian, *Crime and Criminals in Victorian England* (The History Press, 2011)

Hewitt, Eric J., *A History of Policing in Manchester* (E. J. Morten, 1979)

Higgs, Michelle, *Prison Life in Victorian England* (Tempus, 2007)

Schpayer-Makov, Haia, *The Ascent of the Detective: Police Sleuths in Victorian and Edwardian England* (Oxford University Press, 2011)

Wade, Stephen, *Tracing Your Police Ancestors: A Guide for Family Historians* (Pen & Sword, 2009)

Research sources

Newspapers:

Aberdeen Evening Express – 1894

Aberdeen Journal – 1890

Birmingham Daily Post – 1886, 1890, 1895

Blackburn Standard – 1875, 1889

Burnley Express – 1893

Cheshire Observer – 1884

Daily Despatch – 1914

Daily Mail – 1897, 1899, 1914

Daily Telegraph – 1889

Devon and Exeter Daily Gazette – 1890

Gloucester Citizen – 1884

London Standard – 1862

Lancaster Gazette – 1889, 1893

Manchester Courier and Lancashire General Advertiser – 1876, 1884, 1885, 1888, 1889, 1890, 1892, 1893, 1895, 1896, 1897, 1901, 1902, 1903, 1906, 1907, 1908, 1909, 1912, 1913, 1914

Manchester Evening Chronicle – 1899, 1901, 1914

Manchester Evening News – 1874, 1882, 1884, 1886, 1887, 1893, 1894, 1899, 1902, 1903

Manchester Guardian – 1890, 1895, 1896, 1897, 1898, 1899, 1901, 1903, 1907, 1910, 1912, 1914

Manchester Times – 1888, 1890, 1892, 1893

Nottingham Evening Post – 1880, 1882, 1887, 1895

Nottinghamshire Guardian – 1876, 1886
Police Review and Parade Gossip – 1898
Preston Chronicle – 1889
Reynolds's Newspaper – 1881, 1884
Sheffield Daily Telegraph – 1896
Sporting Chronicle – 1885
The Times – 1882, 1889, 1892, 1894, 1897
Western Daily Press – 1926
Worcestershire Chronicle – 1887

Researchers interested in any specific article references are welcome to contact me through my publisher for more details.

Museums and archives:

Greater Manchester Police Museum and Archives
The museum holds an archive about Jerome Caminada, including press cuttings, artefacts, and original copies of his memoirs.

Greater Manchester Police Museum and Archives
57a Newton Street,
Northern Quarter,
Manchester M1 1ET
0161 856 3287/4500
Website: *www.gmpmuseum.com*

Greater Manchester County Record Office and The Manchester Room @ City Library
The archive holds a wide range of material relating to the history of Manchester and family history, including court records, prison records, Poor Law and workhouse records, Watch Committee minute books, as well as parish records and municipal cemetery burial registers.
For further information:
0161 234 1979
Email: archiveslocalstudies@manchester.gov.uk
Website: *www.manchester.gov.uk/info/448*

The British Newspaper Archive
Almost seven million online historical newspaper pages are available to date, with continuing work to digitise up to 40 million from the British Library's vast collection. This invaluable resource includes news articles, family notices, letters, obituaries and advertisements.
Website: *www.britishnewspaperarchive.co.uk*

The National Archives
Home Office files in the series HO144 hold correspondence and reports relating to
Fenian activity during the dynamite campaign of the 1880s.
The National Archives,
Kew,
Richmond,
Surrey TW9 4DU
0208 876 3444
Website: *www.nationalarchives.gov.uk*

Acknowledgements

I have been surprised and delighted by the interest shown in this project and a big thank you to everyone who has joined me along the way. Firstly, I would like to thank my wonderful editor, Jen Newby, who has been an invaluable support and constant friendly presence. The book is considerably better for her incisive comments and suggestions. Special thanks also to my publishers, Pen and Sword Books, for this fantastic opportunity.

Researching the book has been a thoroughly enjoyable experience. I am particularly grateful to Grant Millar at the British Newspaper Archives, for allowing me to use images from the archive. I would also like to express my appreciation to Duncan Broady, curator of the Greater Manchester Police Museum and Archives for sharing information and ideas, as well as kindly permitting me to use the only official surviving image of Jerome Caminada for the cover of the book. In addition, I would like to thank the staff at the Greater Manchester County Record Office and the Manchester Room @ City Library for their assistance.

During the writing of the book, I have been lucky enough to have the excellent company of many writers, historians and genealogists, whom I consider to be friends as well as writing companions. I would especially like to thank Theresa Moran for teaching me about Irish history and Rachael Hale for her encouragement and writerly help: her red pen is second to none.

Finally, I would like to thank Warren, Ella and Ethan for accepting Detective Caminada into our home. I could not have written his story without their unwavering support.

Index

Explore the past with The British Newspaper Archive

The Victorian era was a fascinating period of British history and one recorded in great detail by the newspapers of the day.

Many local and regional newspapers held in the British Library's Newspaper Collection have now been made available to search and view online at www.britishnewspaperarchive.co.uk

Search historical newspapers online

- Over 7 million pages to explore
- Thousands of extra pages added every day
- Newspapers cover 1710 – 1954
- Search by keyword, date, place or newspaper title
- Search for free, then view articles from just £6.95

Discover history as it was written

- Read original reports about historical events
- Investigate forgotten stories from the past
- Uncover amazing details about what life was like
- Explore local, national and international news
- Search news articles, advertisements, recipes and more

Claim 15 credits for free and start exploring The British Newspaper Archive today!

We'll automatically add the free credits to your account when you register at www.britishnewspaperarchive.co.uk/account/register